RECORDED VERSIONS
GUITAR

AUTHENTIC TRANSCRIPTIONS
WITH NOTES AND TABLATURE

GUITAR HERO III

LEGENDS of ROCK

SONGBOOK

Artwork © Activision

Exclusive Distributors:
Music Sales Limited
14-15 Berners Street, London W1T 3LJ, UK.

Order No. HLE90003694
ISBN 978-1-84772-790-9
This book © Copyright 2008 Hal Leonard Europe

Printed in the USA

Your Guarantee of Quality
As publishers, we strive to produce every book to the highest commercial standards.
The book has been carefully designed to minimise awkward page turns and to make playing from it a real pleasure.
Throughout, the printing and binding have been planned to ensure a sturdy, attractive publication which should give years of enjoyment.
If your copy fails to meet our high standards, please inform us and we will gladly replace it.

www.musicsales.com

Anarchy In The U.K.

Words and Music by John Lydon, Paul Cook, Stephen Jones and Glen Matlock

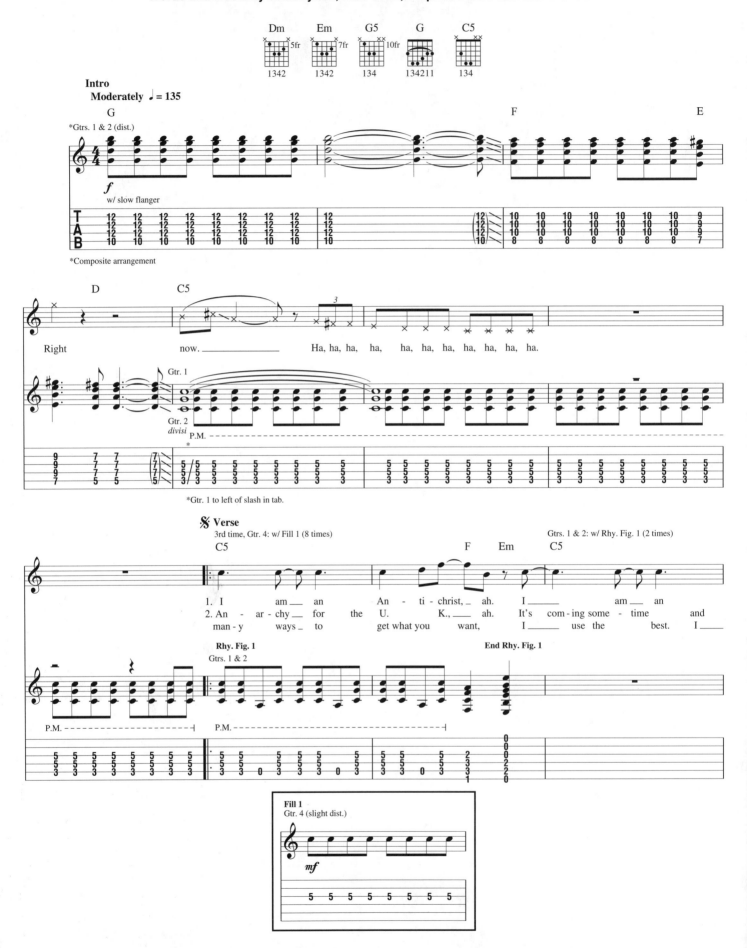

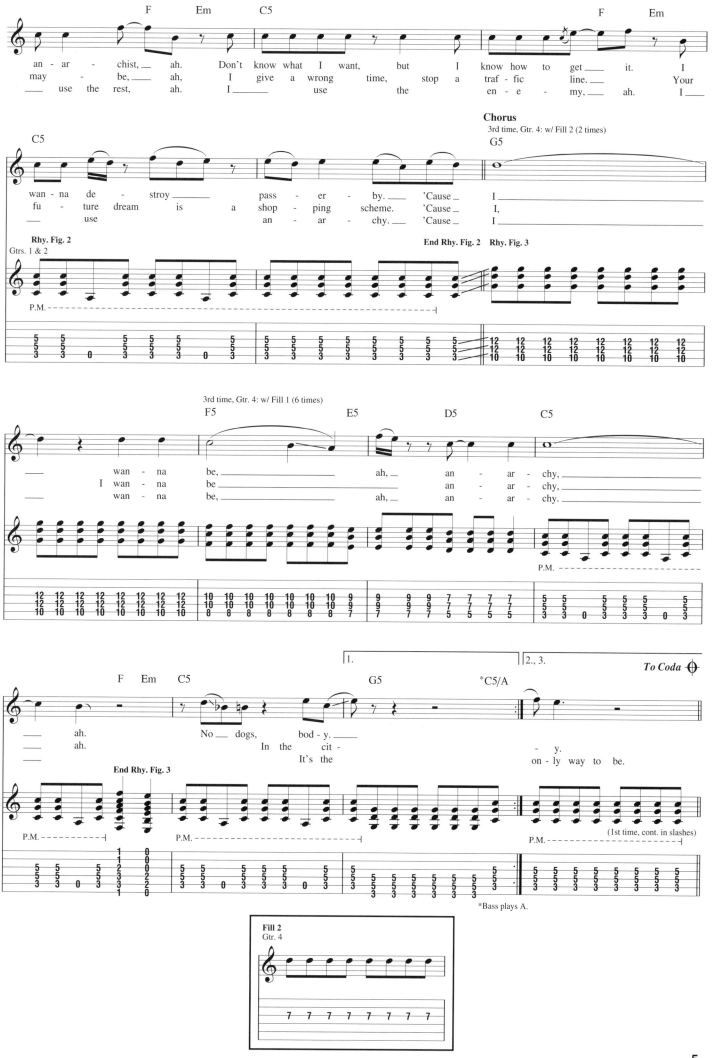

Guitar Solo

*See top of first page of song for chord diagrams pertaining to rhythm slashes.

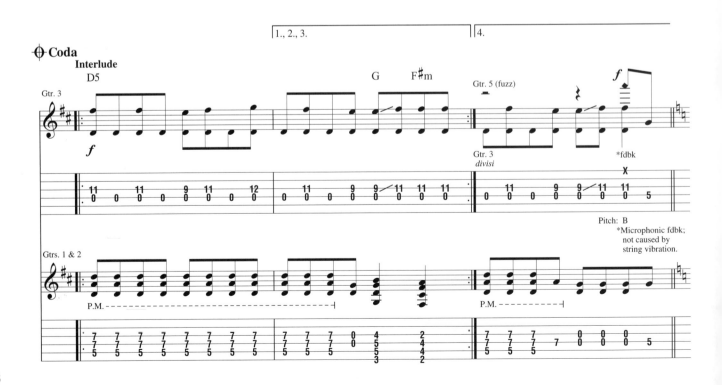

Verse

Gtrs. 1 & 2: w/ Rhy. Fig. 1 (3 times)
Gtr. 3 tacet

4. Is this __ the M. P. L. A., __ ah, or is this __ the U. D. A., __ ah, or is this __ the I. R. A., __ ah? I __

Pitch: G

Outro-Chorus

Gtrs. 1 & 2: w/ Rhy. Fig. 2

Gtrs. 1 & 2: w/ Rhy. Fig. 3

__ thought __ it was the U. K. __ or just _____ an - oth - er _____ coun -

Pitch: C

Gtrs. 1 & 2: w/ Rhy. Fig. 2

try. _____

An - oth - er coun - cil ten - an - cy. __

7

Barracuda

Words and Music by Nancy Wilson, Ann Wilson, Michael Derosier and Roger Fisher

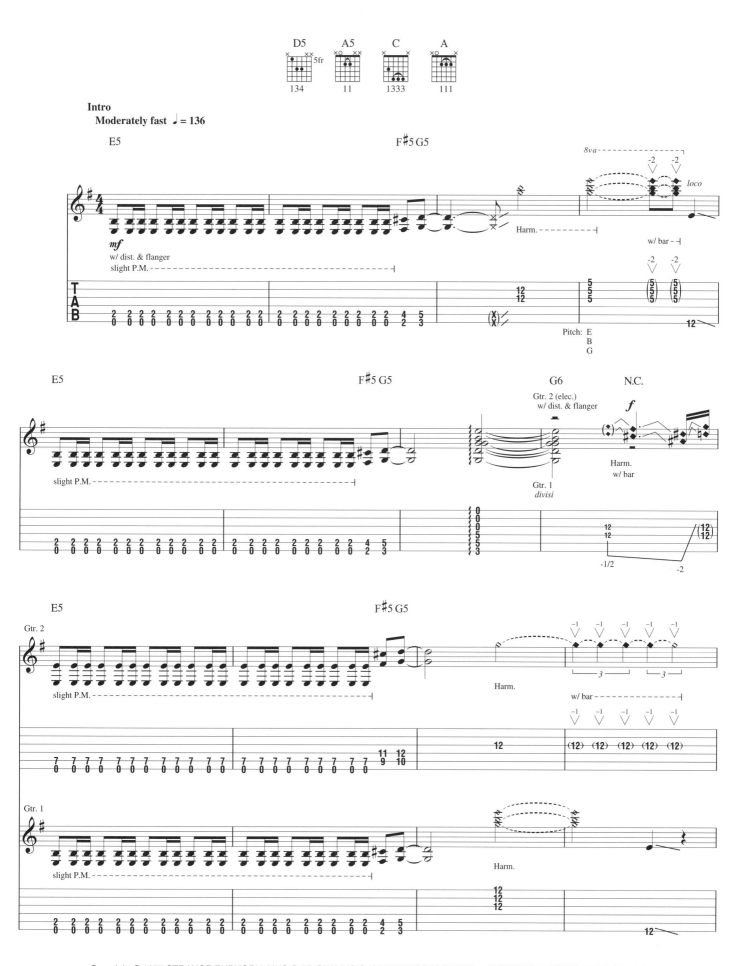

13

⊕ Coda 2

Interlude

Gtrs. 1 & 2: w/ Rhy. Figs. 1 & 1A

E5

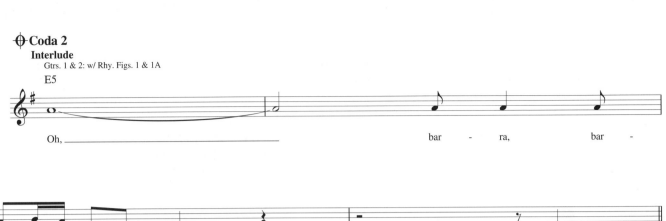

Oh, _____ bar - ra, bar -

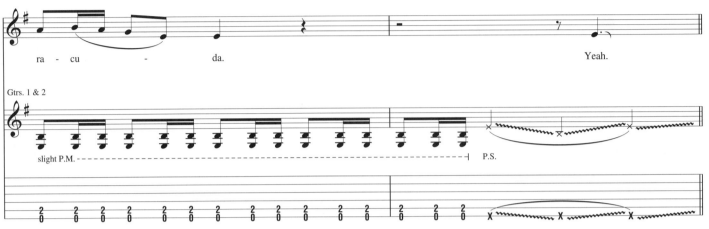

ra - cu - da. Yeah.

Gtrs. 1 & 2

slight P.M. - P.S.

Outro

Gtr. 4: w/ Fill 1

Em7

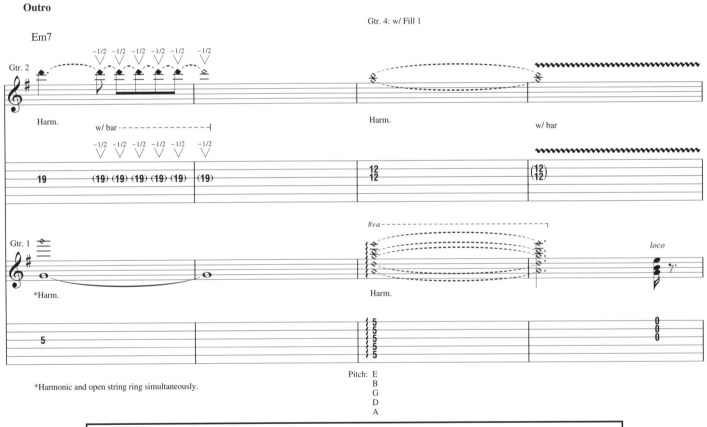

*Harmonic and open string ring simultaneously.

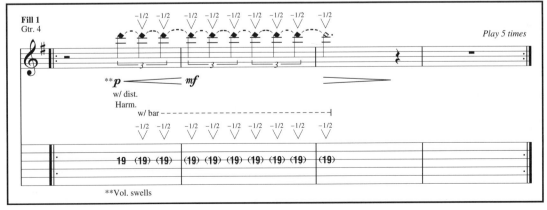

**Vol. swells

16

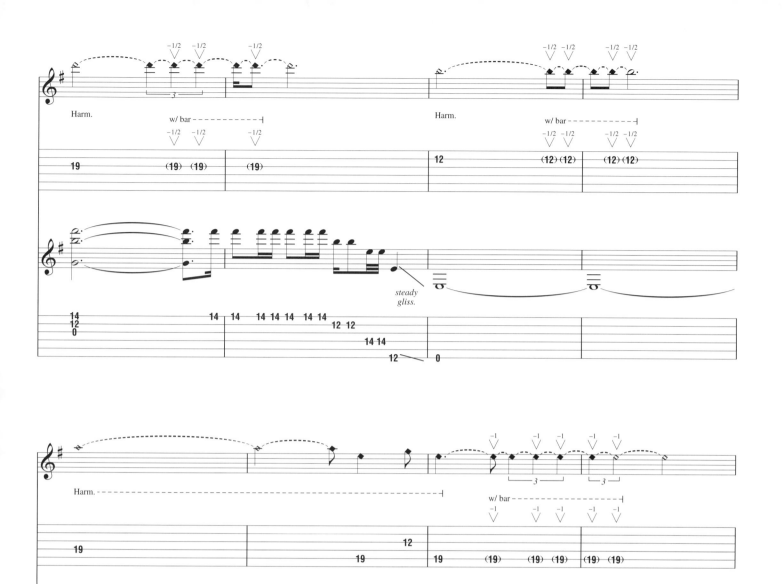

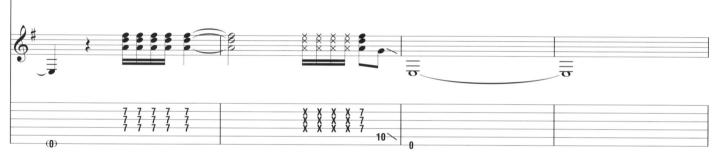

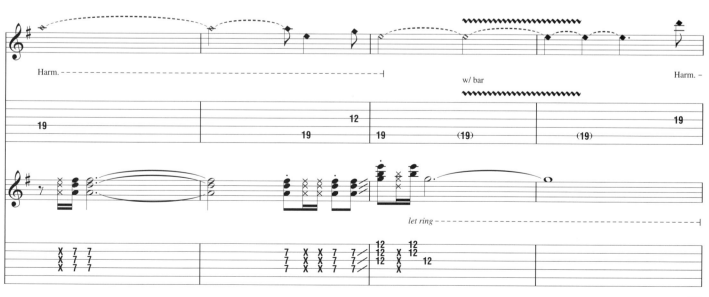

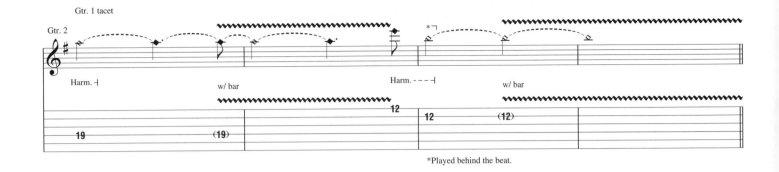

*Played behind the beat.

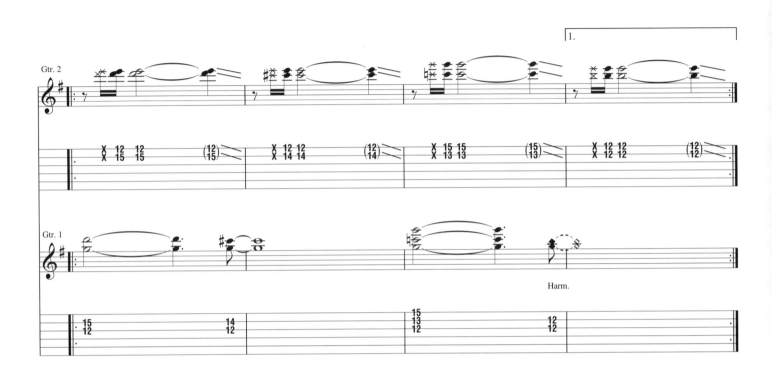

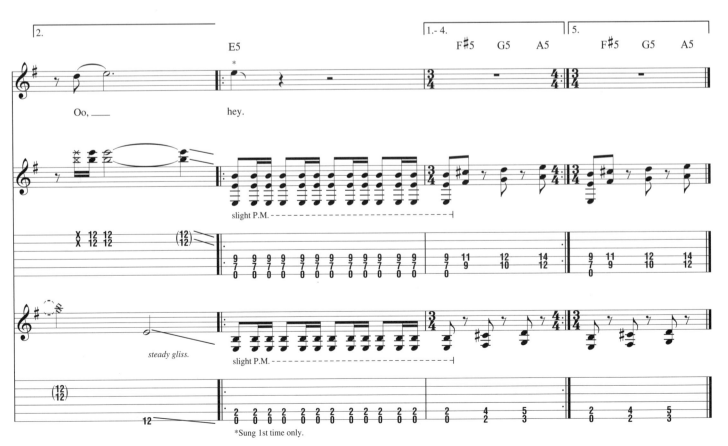

*Sung 1st time only.

Cherub Rock

Words and Music by William Corgan

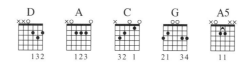

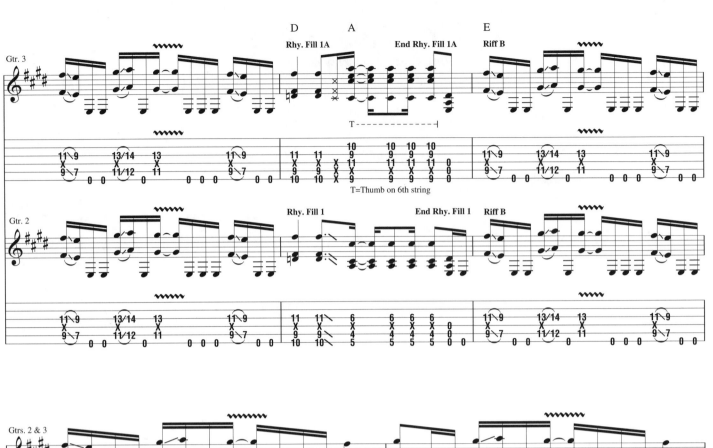

T=Thumb on 6th string

Verse

1. Freak   out,   (and) give   in,   does-n't mat-
sters   u - nite;   come a - lign __

- ter what you be - lieve in.   Stay   cool,   and be __
__ for the big fight __ to rock __ for you. (But) be - ware,   all those an -

Bridge

Gtrs. 2 & 3: w/ Rhy. Figs. 2 & 2A (4 times)

Tell me all _____ of your se - crets. _____ Can-not help _____ but be -

Gtr. 6 (dist.)

fdbk.

Gtr. 7 (dist.)

lieve _____ this __ is true. _____ Tell me all _____ of your se - crets. I know, _

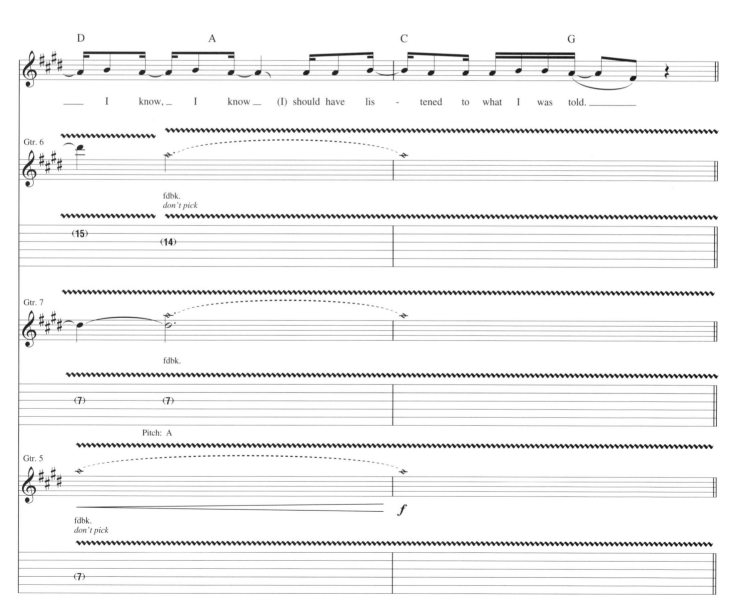

_____ I know, _ I know _ (I) should have lis - tened to what I was told. _____

Chorus

Gtrs. 2 & 3: w/ Rhy. Figs. 2 & 2A (2 times)
Gtr. 4: w/ Rhy. Fig. 3 (2 times)
Gtrs. 6 & 7 tacet

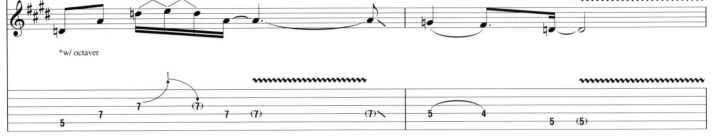

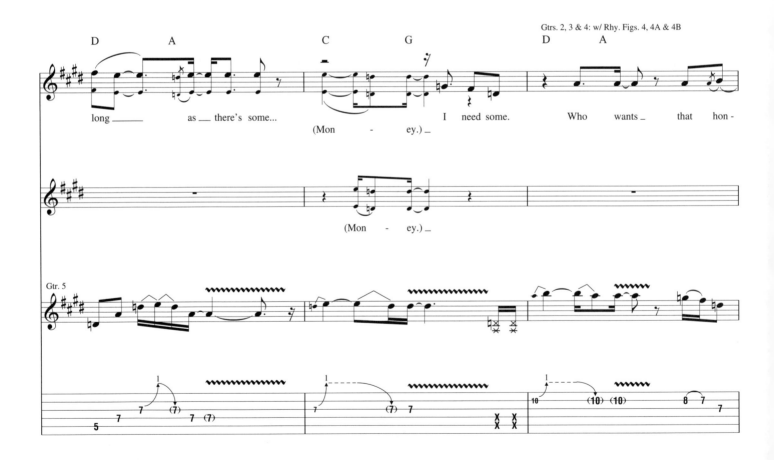

Cities On Flame With Rock 'N' Roll

Words and Music by Samuel Pearlman, Donald Roeser and Albert Bouchard

Cliffs Of Dover

By Eric Johnson

Cult Of Personality

Words and Music by William Calhoun, Corey Glover, Muzz Skillings and Vernon Reid

(Malcom X) *Spoken:* "And during the few moments that we have left... We want to talk right down to earth in a language that everybody here can easily understand."

*Key signature denotes G Dorian.

**Chord symbols reflect basic harmony.

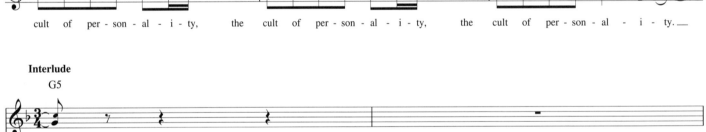

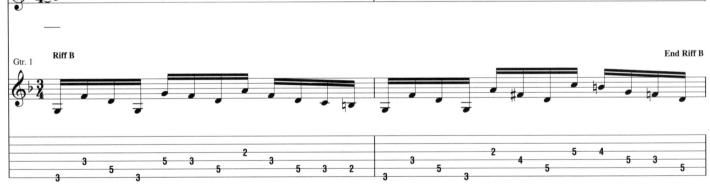

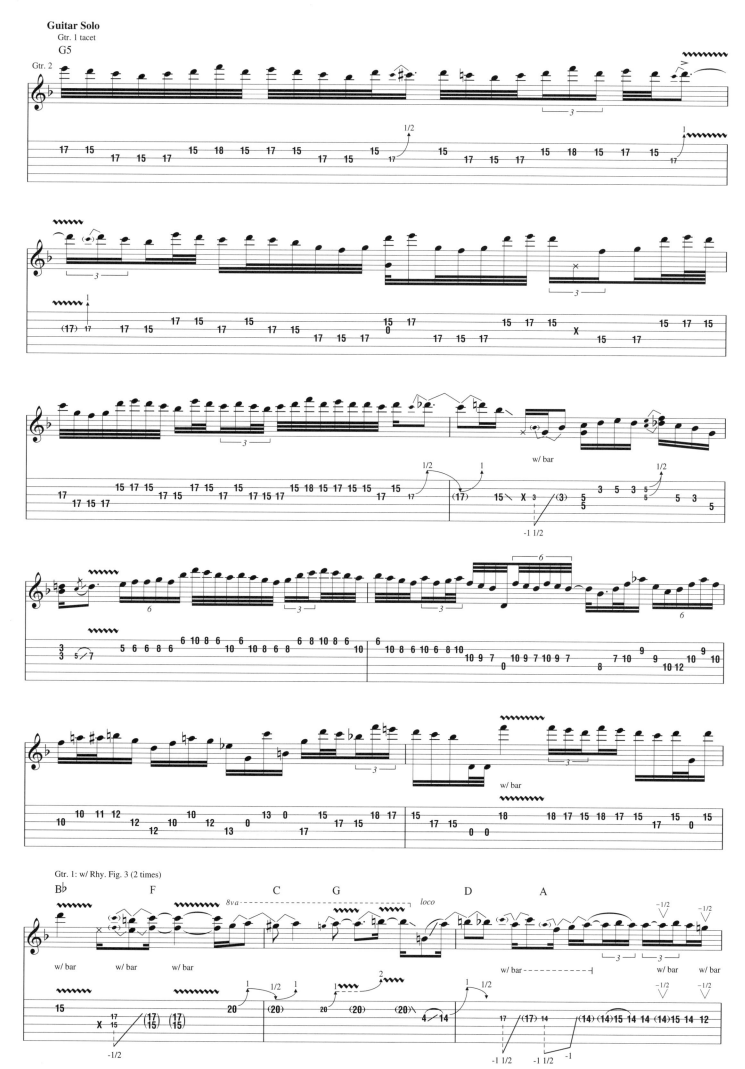

3. You gave me for - tune, you gave me fame.

The Devil Went Down To Georgia

Words and Music by Charlie Daniels, John Thomas Crain, Jr., William Joel DiGregorio, Fred Laroy Edwards, Charles Fred Hayward and James Wainwright Marshall

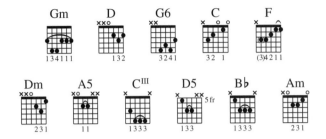

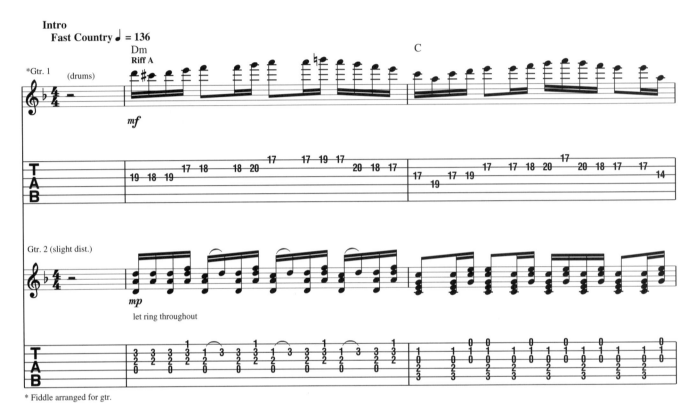

* Fiddle arranged for gtr.

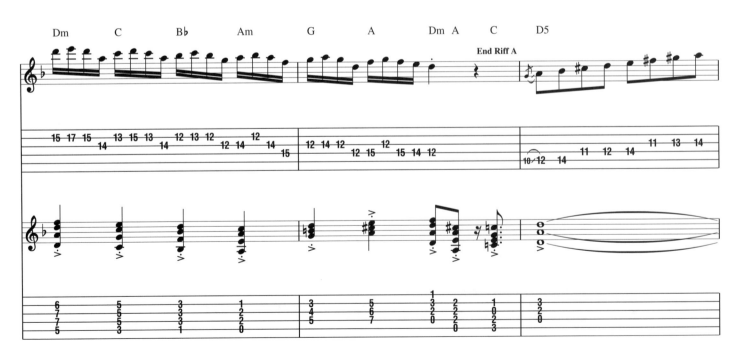

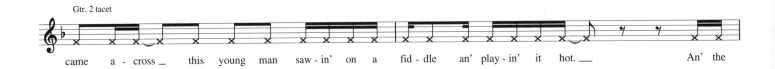

came a-cross this young man saw-in' on a fid - dle an' play-in' it hot. ___ An' the

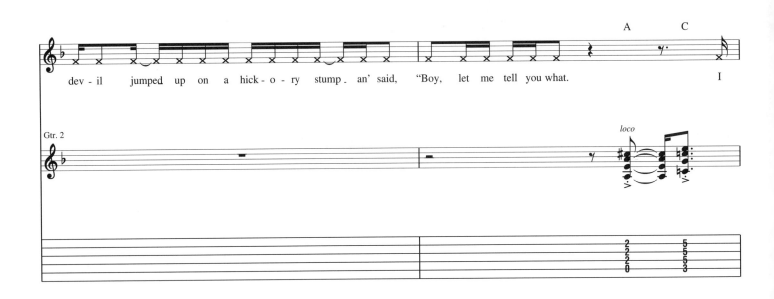

dev - il jumped up on a hick - o - ry stump. an' said, "Boy, let me tell you what. I

guess you did - n't know it, but I'm a fid - dle play - er too. An'

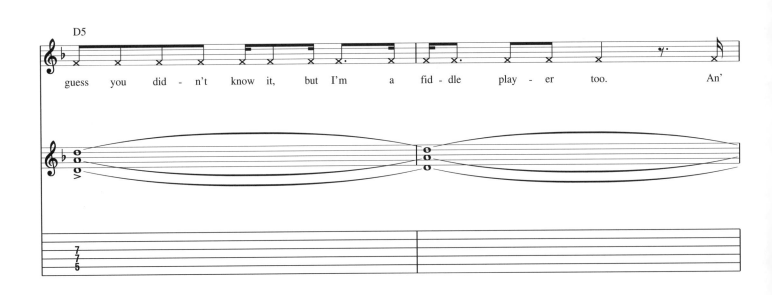

if you'd care to take a dare, ___ I'll make a bet ___ with you. Now,

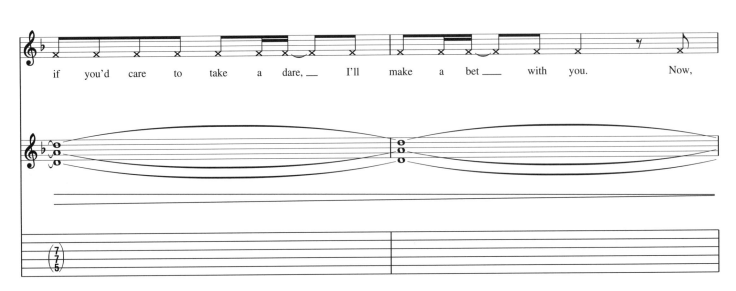

you play pret-ty good fid-dle, boy, __ but give the Dev-il his due. I'll bet a

fid-dle of gold a-gainst your soul, 'cause I think I'm bet-ter than you." The

boy said, "My name's John-ny, an' it might be a sin, __ but I'll

take your bet, you're gon-na re-gret, __ 'cause I'm the best that's ev-er been."__

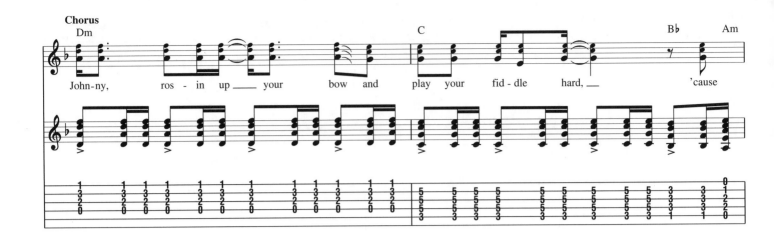

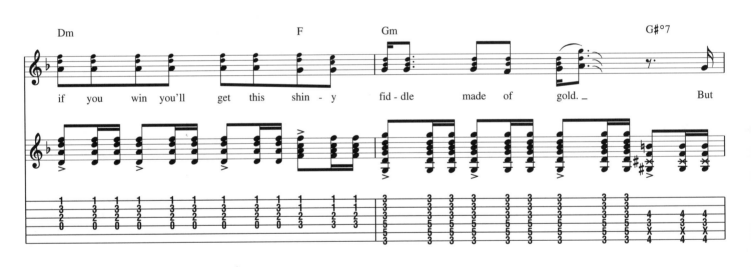

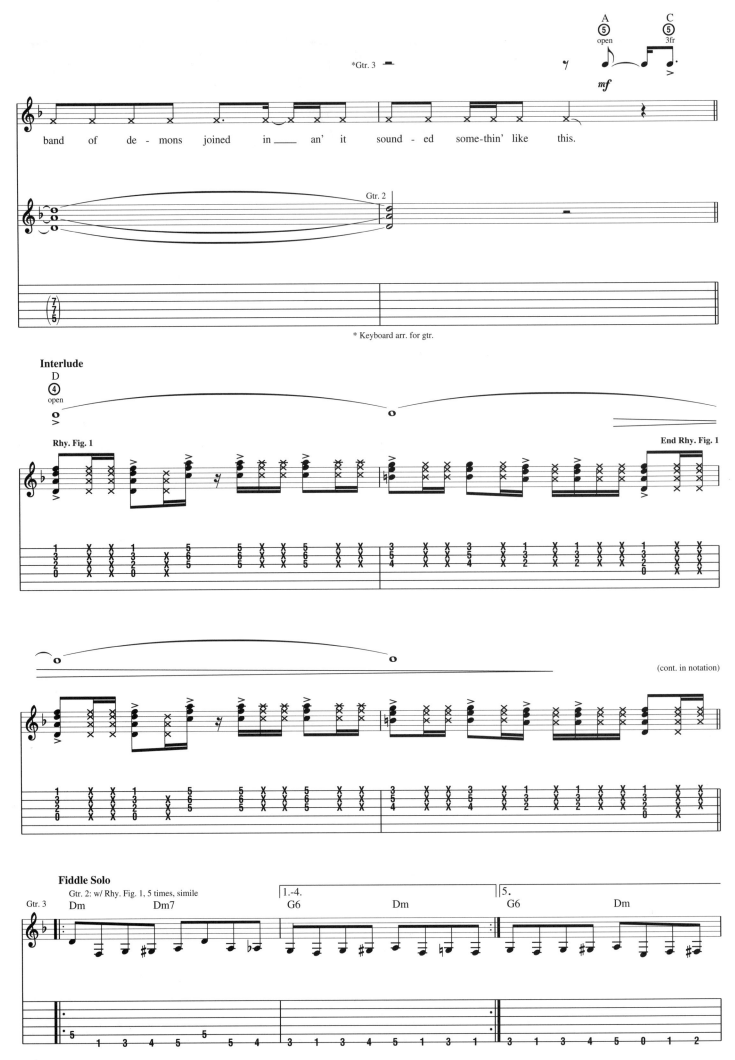

band of de - mons joined in ___ an' it sound - ed some-thin' like this.

* Keyboard arr. for gtr.

Interlude

Fiddle Solo

Spoken: 3. When the

* Ties apply to Gtr. 3 only.

Verse

dev - il fin - ished, John - ny said, __ "Well, you're pret - ty good __ old son, but

sit down in that chair right there an' let me show you how it's done."

Gran-ny does your dog bite? No, child, no.

Verse

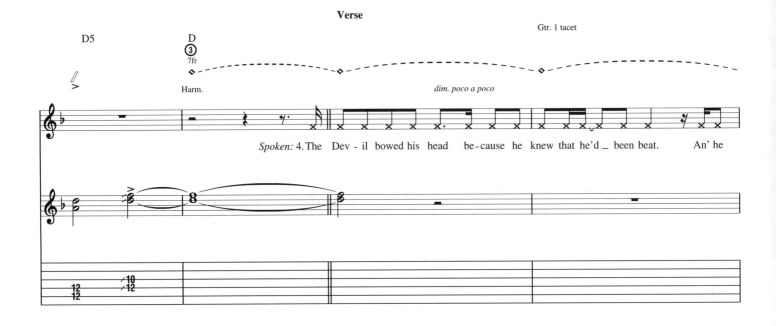

Spoken: 4. The Dev - il bowed his head be - cause he knew that he'd _ been beat. An' he

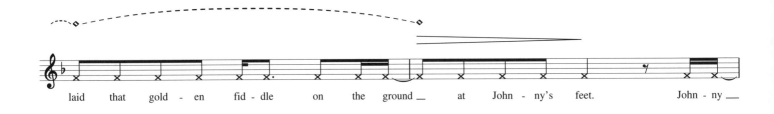

laid that gold - en fid - dle on the ground _ at John - ny's feet. John - ny _

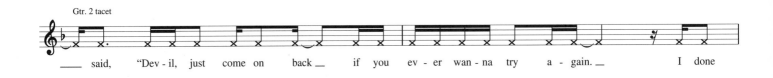

_ said, "Dev - il, just come on back _ if you ev - er wan - na try a - gain. _ I done

told you once, you son of a bitch, _ I'm the best that's ev - er been." _ He played.

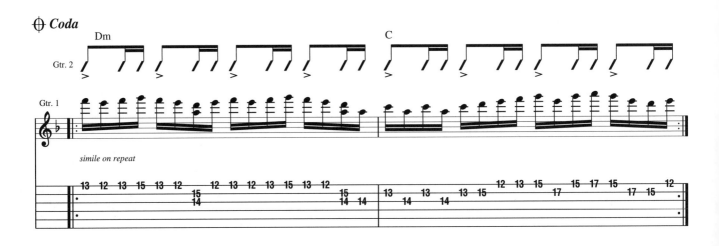

simile on repeat

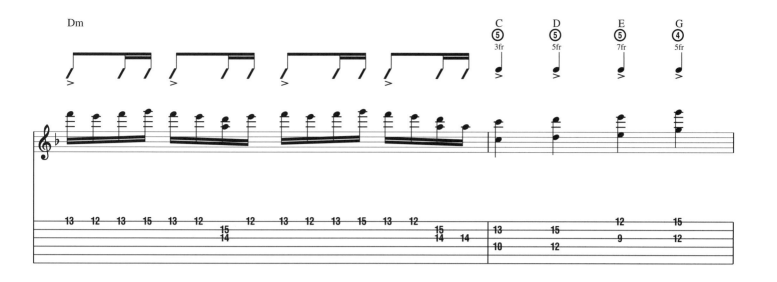

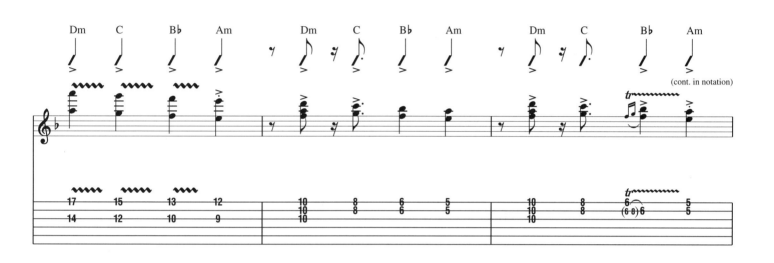

(cont. in notation)

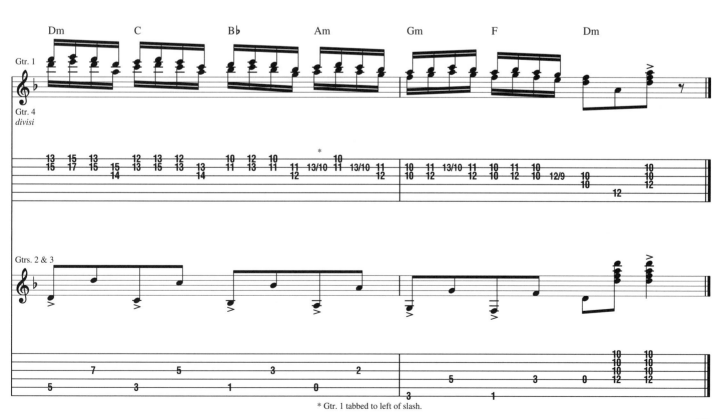

* Gtr. 1 tabbed to left of slash.

Even Flow

Music by Stone Gossard
Lyric by Eddie Vedder

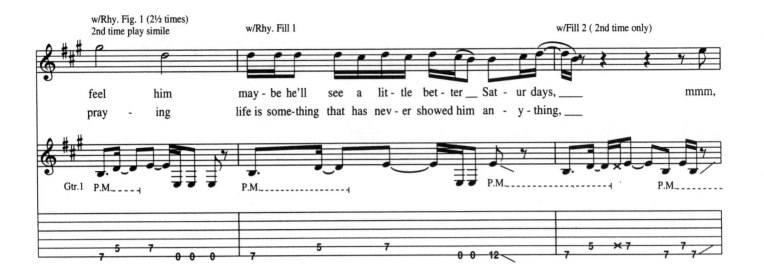

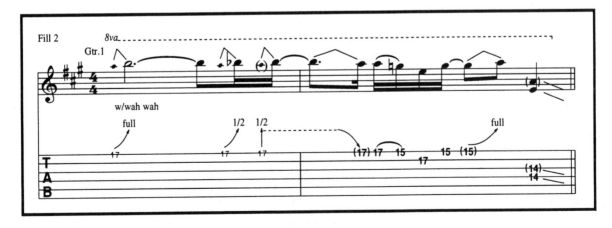

1.

Chorus

E - ven __ flow, ____   thoughts ar - rive like   but - ter - flies. __   Oh,

To Coda ⊕

Spoken: Funk it up

Guitar Solo

N.C.

Rhy. Fig. 3

(end Rhy. Fig. 3)

* Simultaneously play lower note with pick and upper note with middle finger

Hit Me With Your Best Shot

Words and Music by Eddie Schwartz

72

Holiday In Cambodia

Words and Music by Bruce Slesinger, Darren Henley, East Bay Ray, Jello Biafra and Klaus Flouride

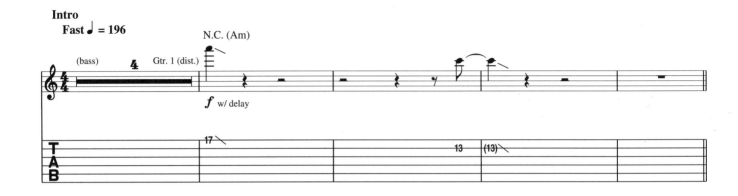

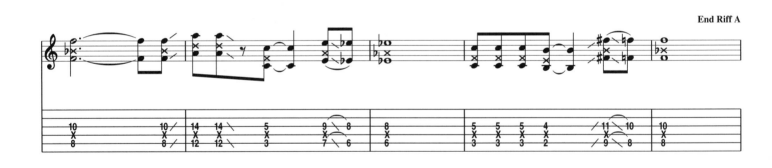

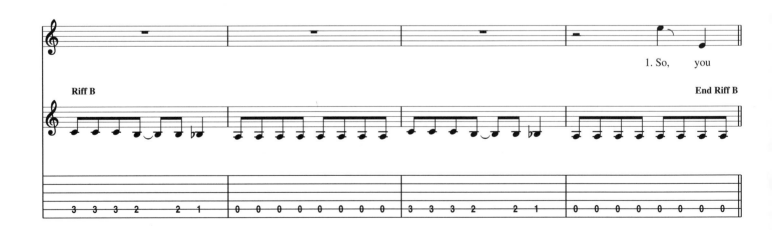

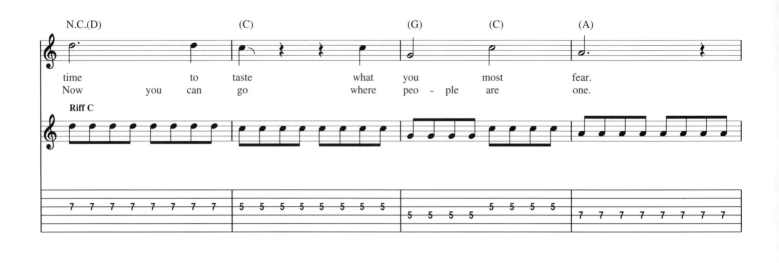

time to taste what you most fear.
Now you can go where people are one.

Riff C

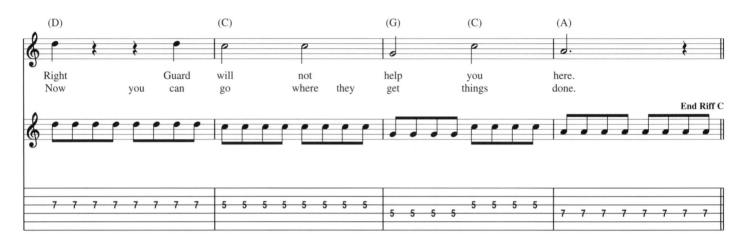

Right Guard will not help you here.
Now you can go where they get things done.

End Riff C

Pre-Chorus

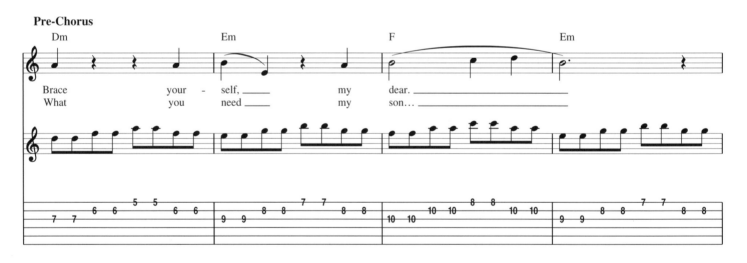

Brace your-self, _____ my dear. _____
What you need _____ my son... _____

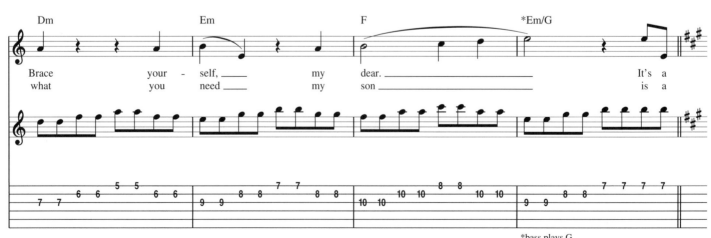

Brace your-self, _____ my dear. _____ It's a
what you need _____ my son _____ is a

*bass plays G

*Slide down string while picking.
Pitches and TAB numbers are approx.

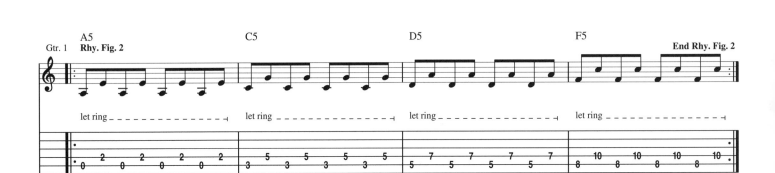

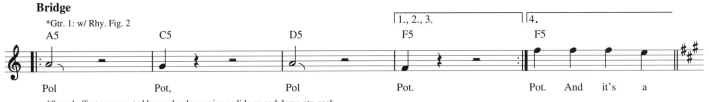

Bridge

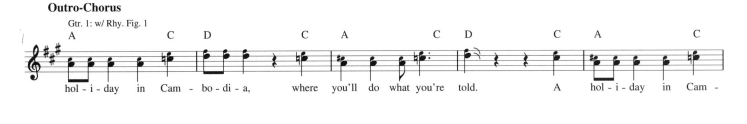

*Sound effects are created by randomly running a slide up and down gtr. neck.

Outro-Chorus

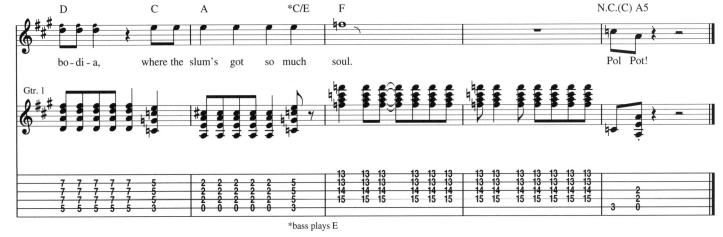

*bass plays E

La Grange

Words and Music by Billy F Gibbons, Dusty Hill and Frank Lee Beard

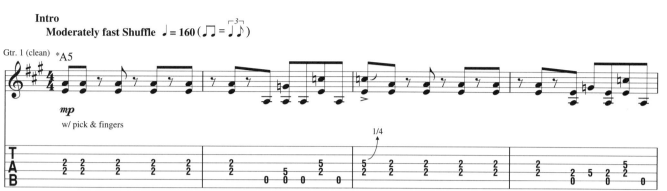

*Chord symbols reflect basic harmony.

Ru - mour spread - in' 'round,

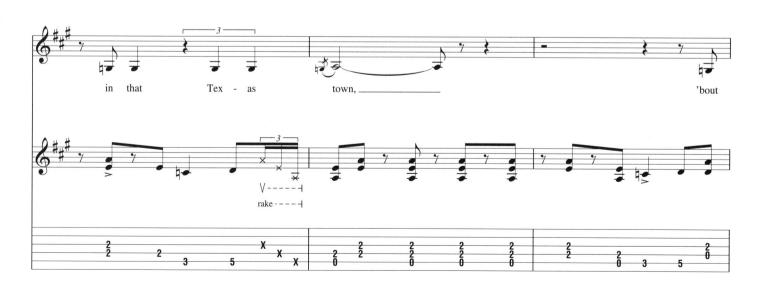

in that Tex - as town, _____ 'bout

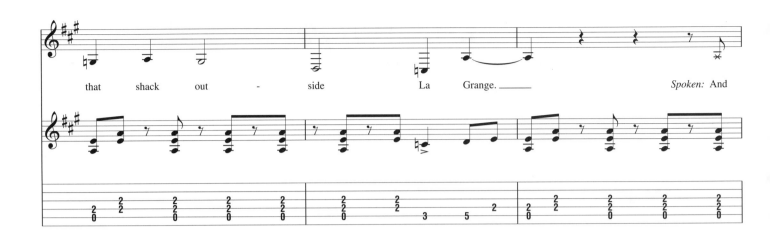

that shack out - side La Grange. _____ *Spoken:* And

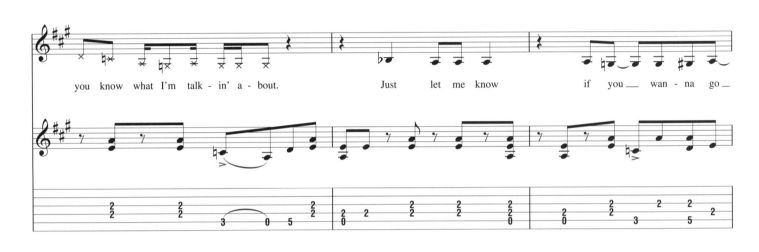

you know what I'm talk - in' a - bout. Just let me know if you __ wan - na go __

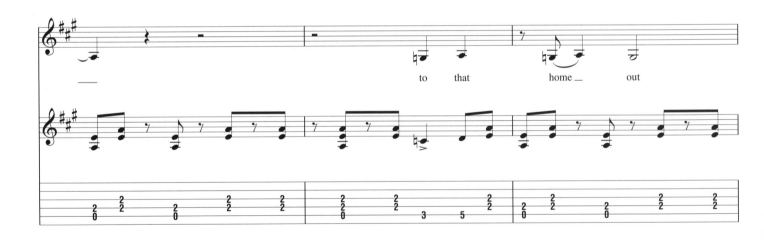

to that home __ out

on __ the range. *Spoken:* They got - ta lot - ta nice girls.

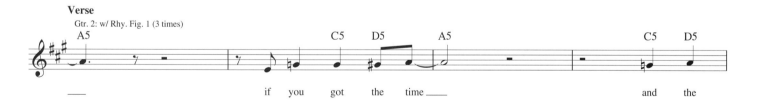

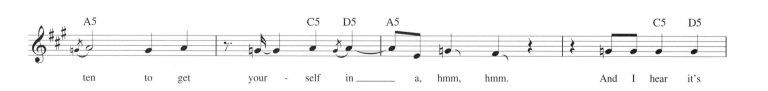

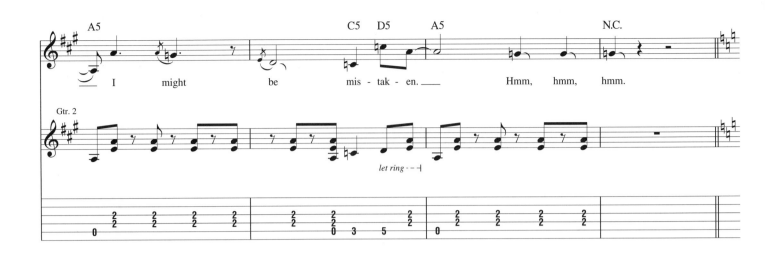

I might be mis - tak - en. _____ Hmm, hmm, hmm.

Guitar Solo

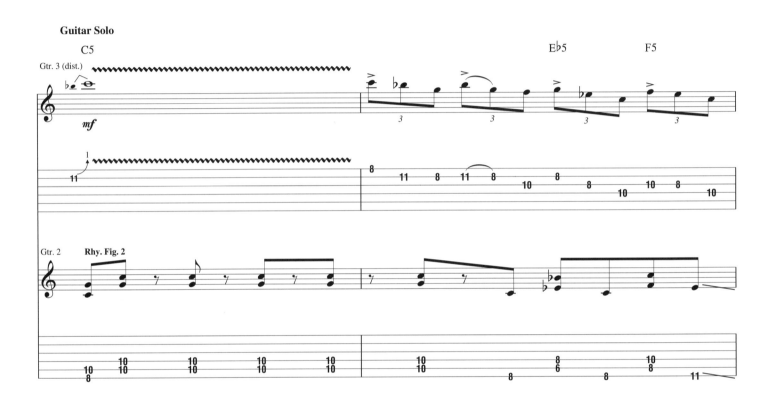

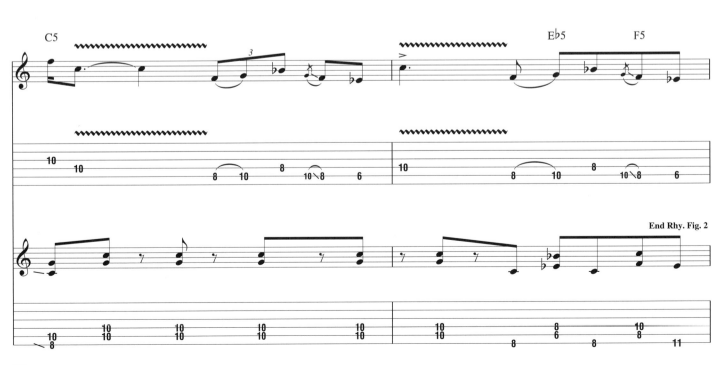

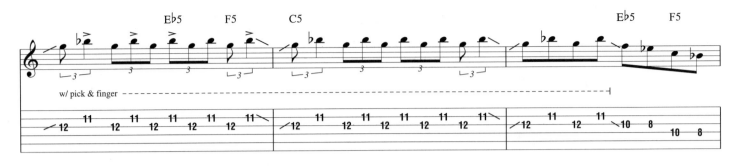

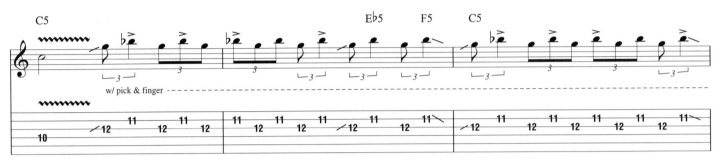

Interlude

*Composite arrangement

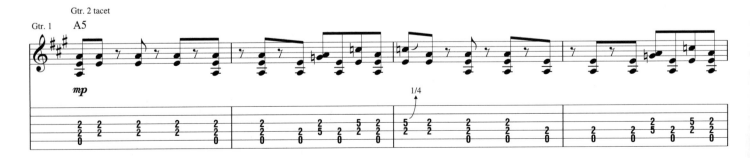

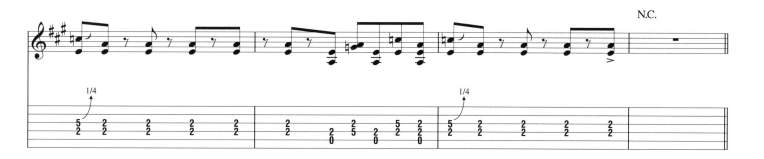

Outro-Guitar Solo

Gtr. 1 tacet

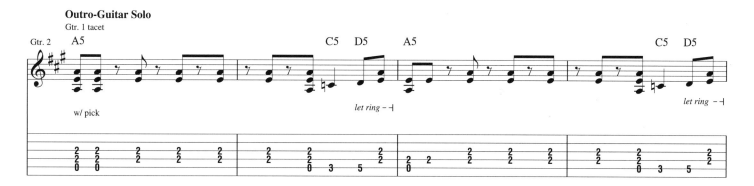

Gtr. 2: w/ Rhy. Fig. 1 (till fade)

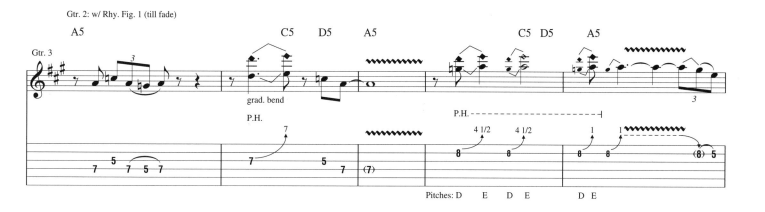

Pitches: D E D E D E

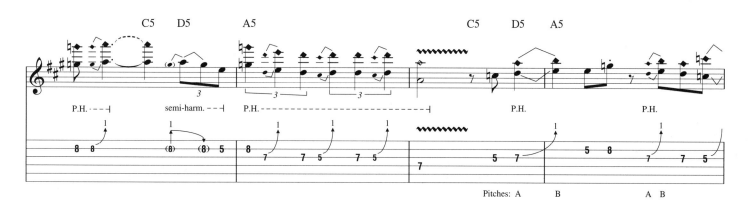

Pitches: A B A B

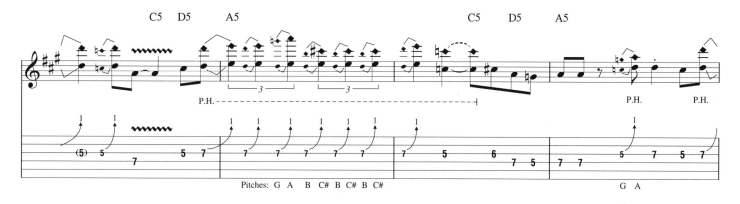

Pitches: G A B C# B C# B C# G A

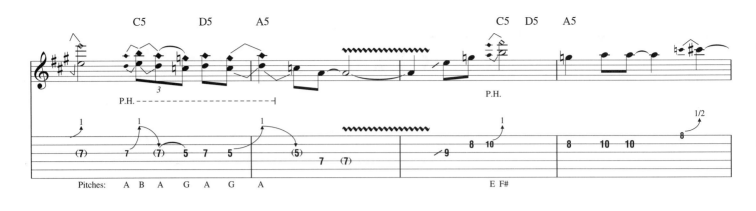

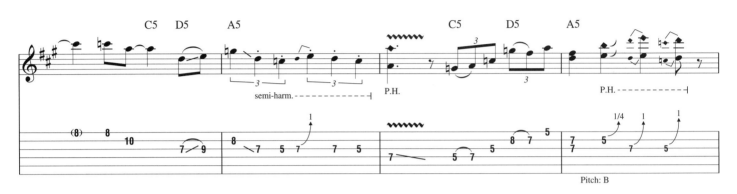

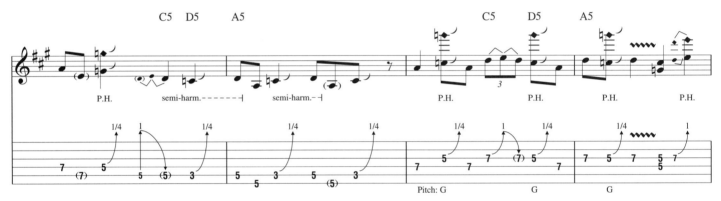

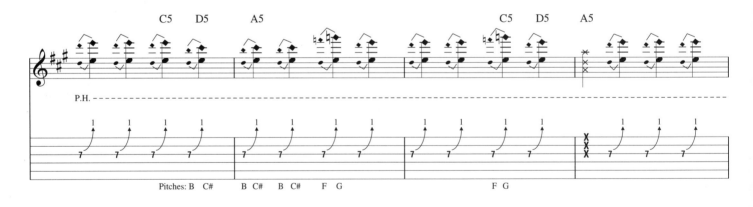

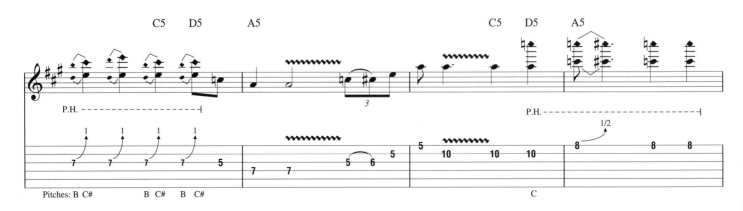

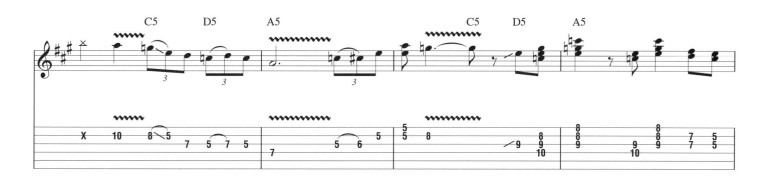

Mississippi Queen

Words and Music by Leslie West, Felix Pappalardi, Corky Laing and David Rea

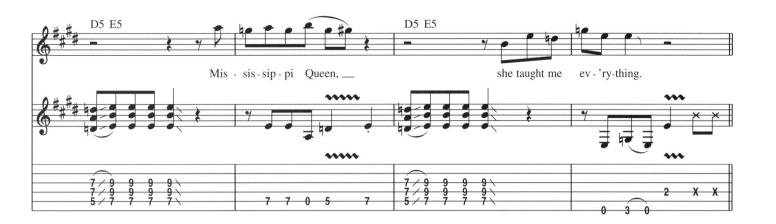

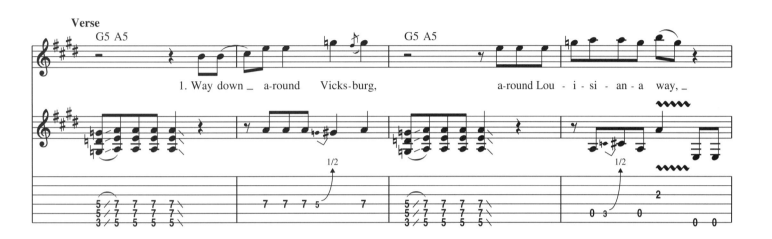

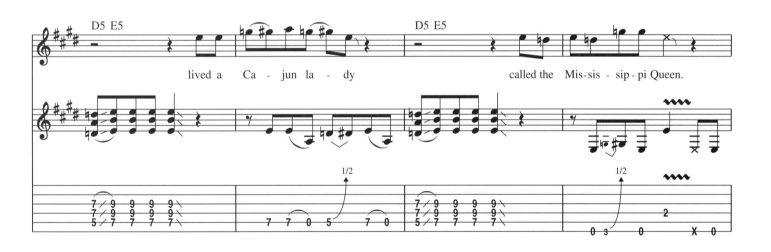

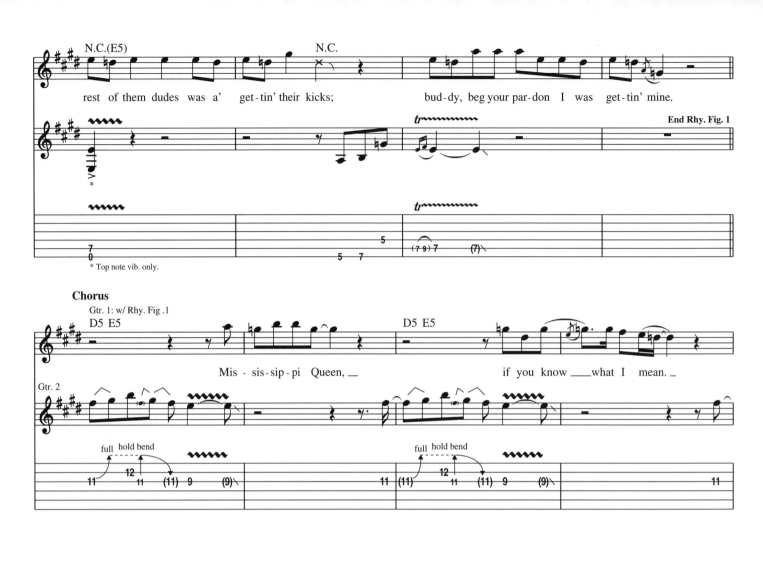

rest of them dudes was a' get-tin' their kicks; bud-dy, beg your par-don I was get-tin' mine.

End Rhy. Fig. 1

* Top note vib. only.

Chorus

Gtr. 1: w/ Rhy. Fig .1

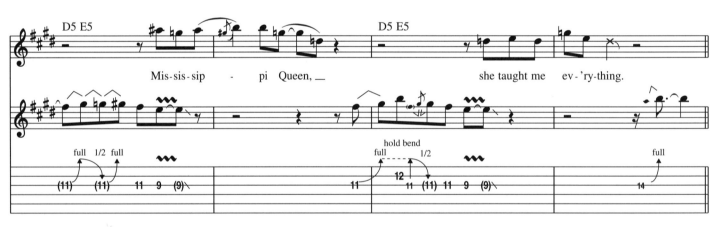

Mis-sis-sip-pi Queen, __ if you know __ what I mean. __

Gtr. 2

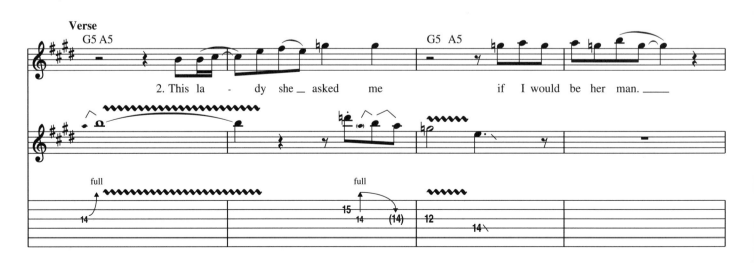

Mis-sis-sip - pi Queen, __ she taught me ev-'ry-thing.

Verse

2. This la - dy she __ asked me if I would be her man. ____

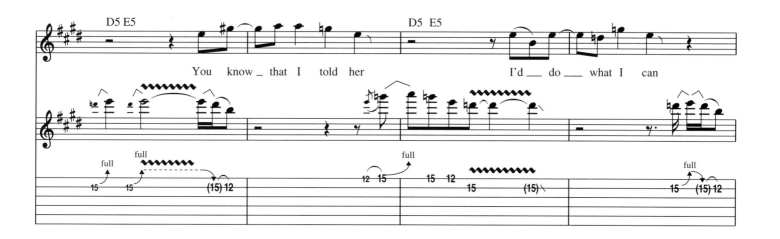

You know ___ that I told her ___ I'd ___ do ___ what I can

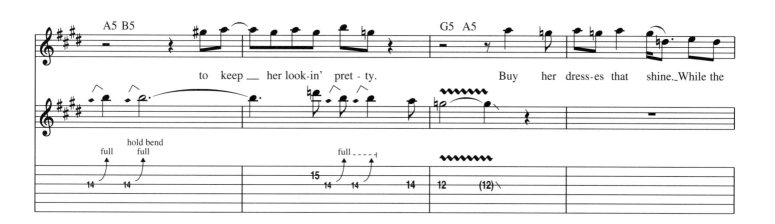

to keep ___ her look-in' pret - ty. Buy her dress-es that shine.__While the

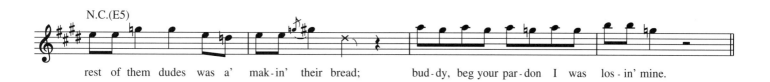

rest of them dudes was a' mak-in' their bread; bud-dy, beg your par-don I was los-in' mine.

Guitar Solo

Gtr. 1: w/ Rhy. Fig. 1, 1st 23 meas. only

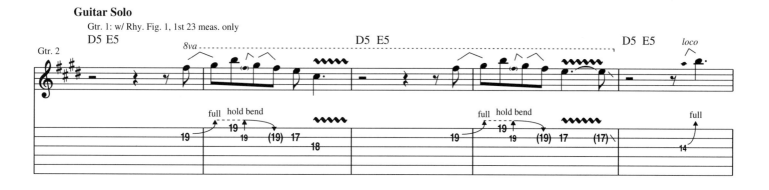

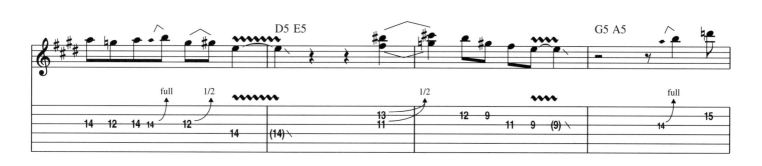

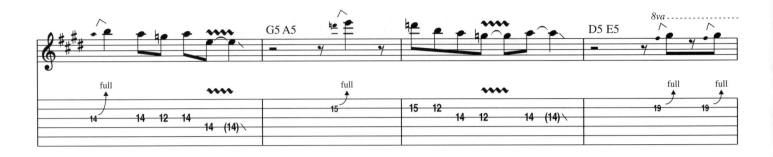

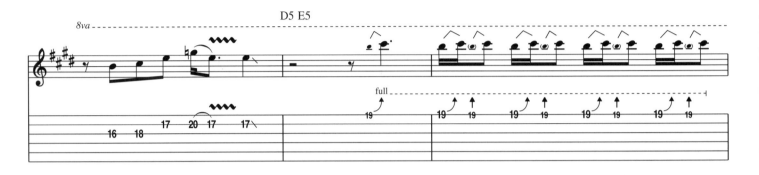

You know _ she was a danc - er, _ she moved _ bet - ter on wine. While the

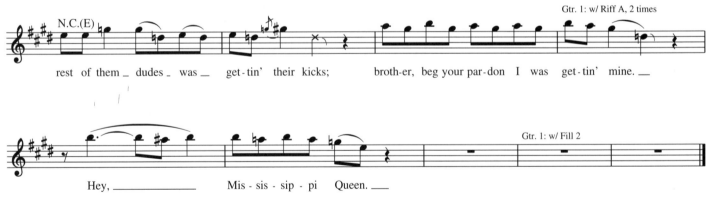

rest of them _ dudes _ was _ get - tin' their kicks; broth - er, beg your par - don I was get - tin' mine. _

Hey, _____ Mis - sis - sip - pi Queen. _

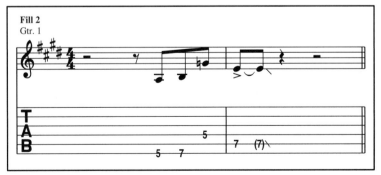

Fill 2
Gtr. 1

My Name Is Jonas

Words and Music by Rivers Cuomo, Jason Cropper and Patrick Wilson

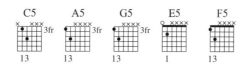

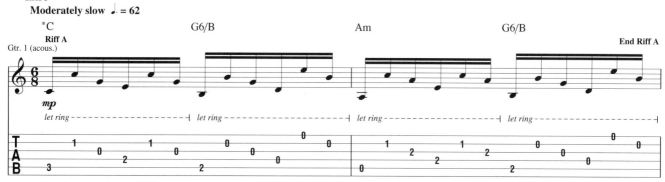

*Chord symbols reflect implied harmony.

Pitch: E
**Vol. swell

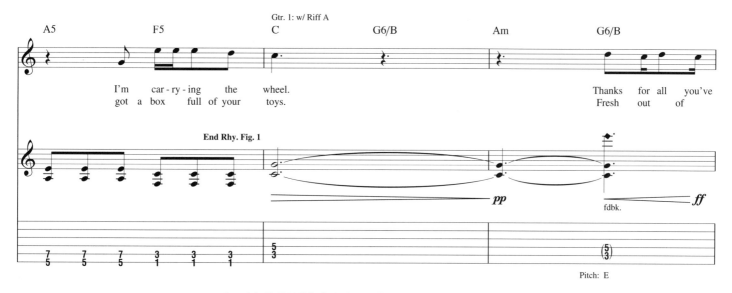

Pitch: E

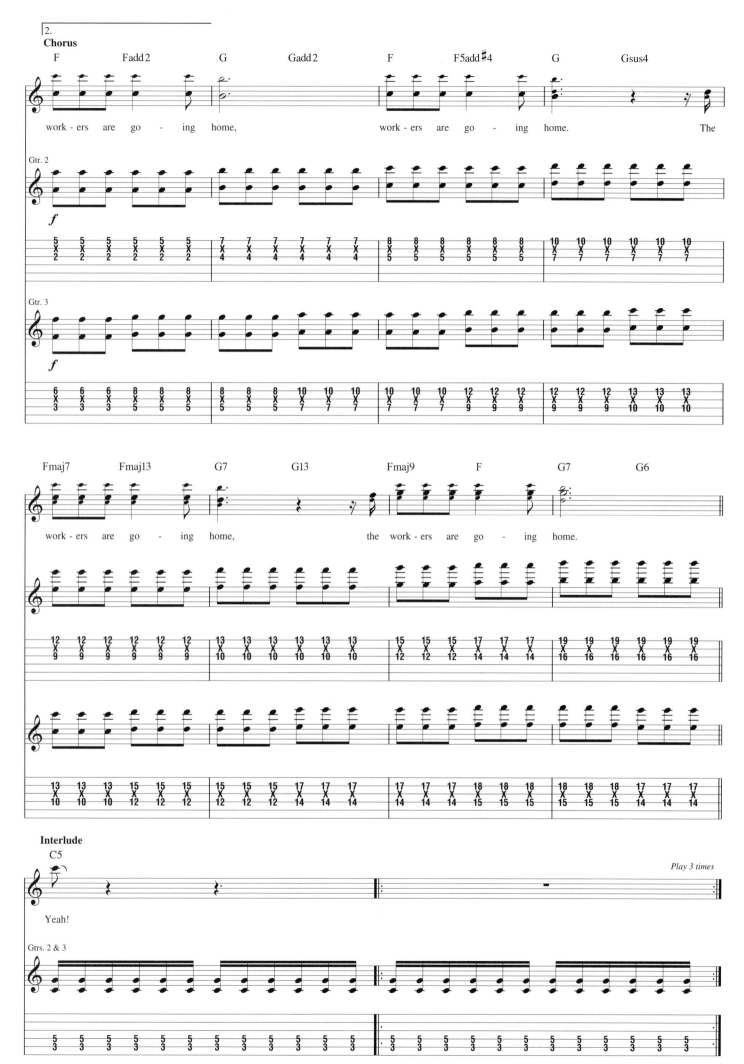

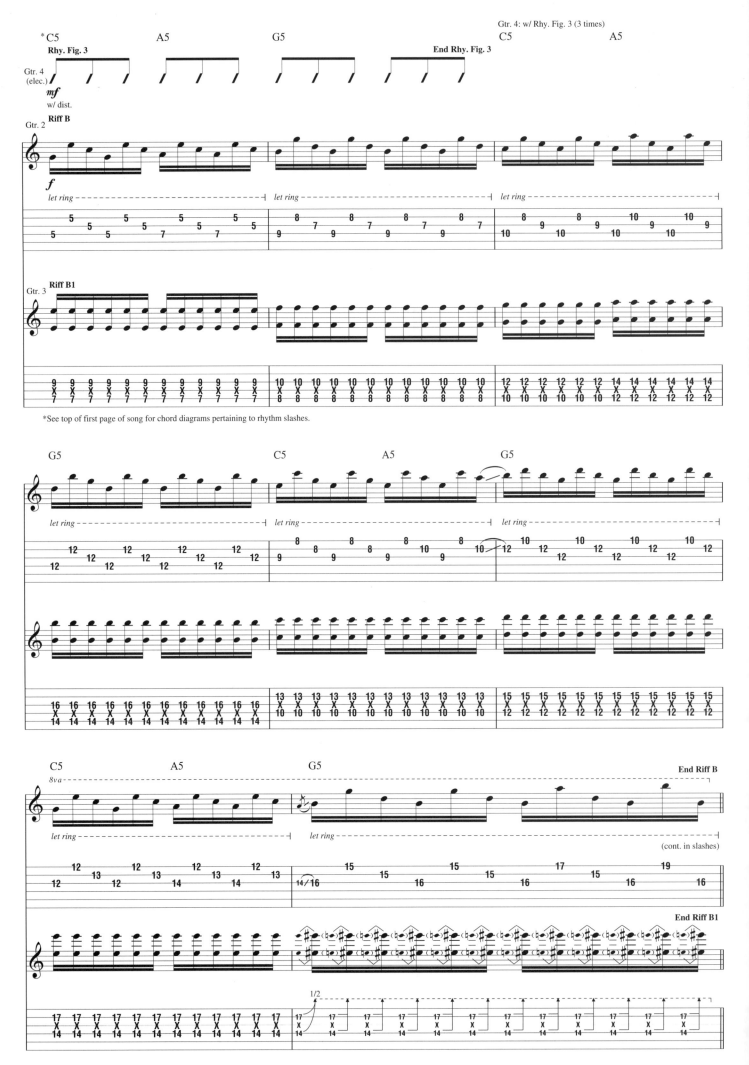

*See top of first page of song for chord diagrams pertaining to rhythm slashes.

One

Words and Music by James Hetfield and Lars Ulrich

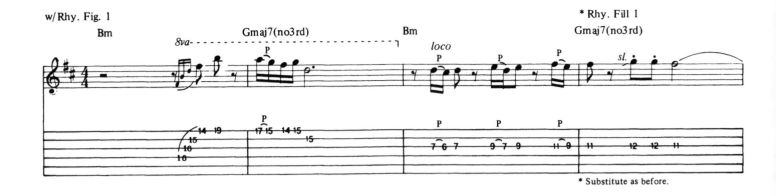

* Substitute as before.

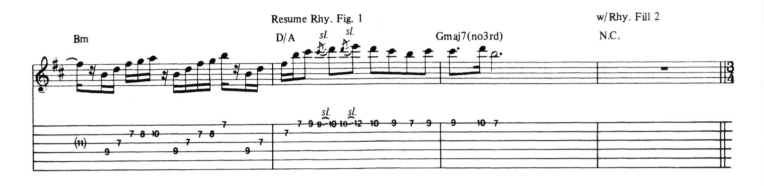

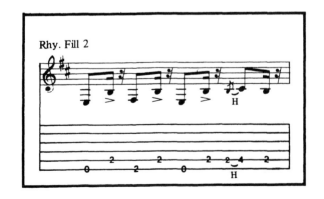

Rhy. Fill 2

1. I can't re-mem-ber an - y - thing,— can't tell if this is true or— dream.
2.Back in the womb it's much too real,— in pumps life that I must— feel,

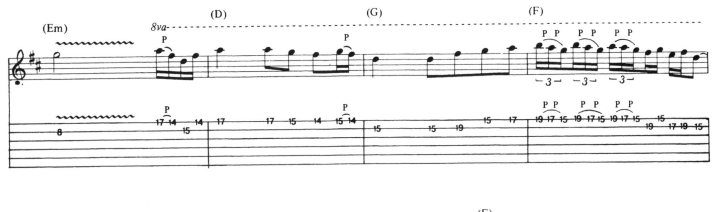

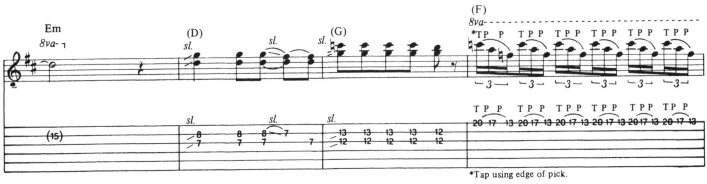

*Tap using edge of pick.

*Silent taps.

Now the world is gone, I'm just one.___ Oh God, help me.

Hold my breath as I wish for death.___ Oh please God, help me!_____

*Downstemmed notes
indicated to right of slash in TAB.

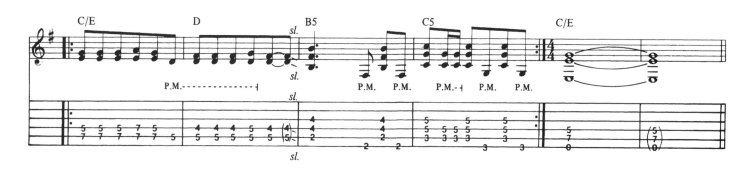

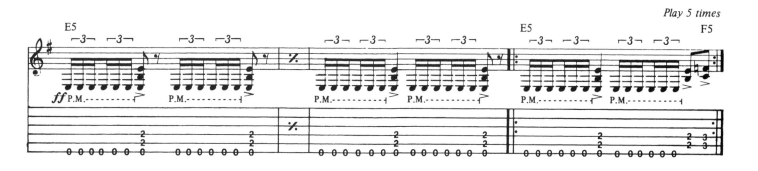

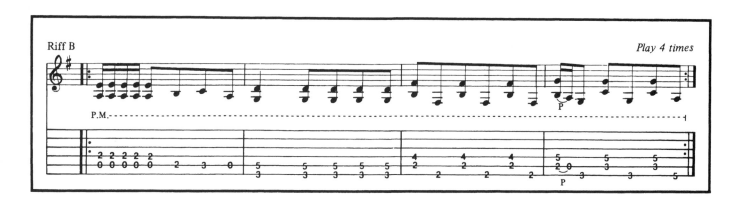

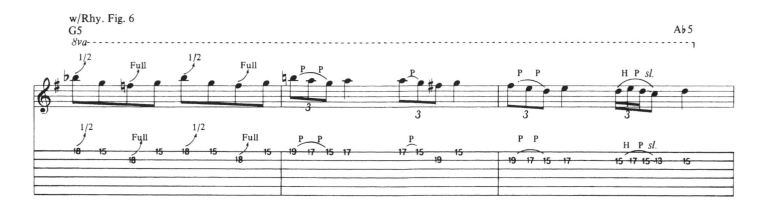

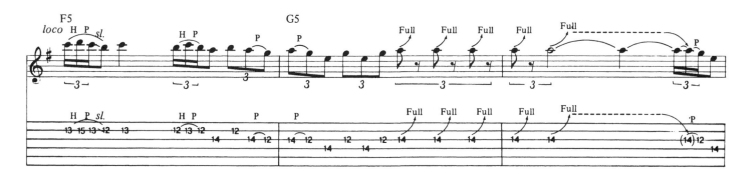

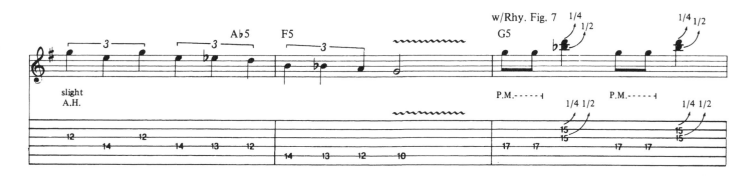

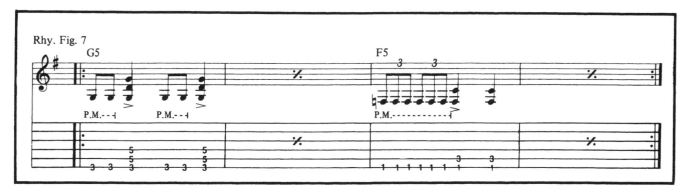

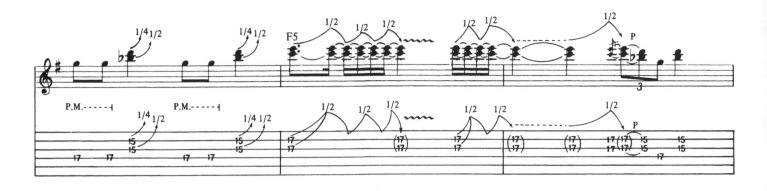

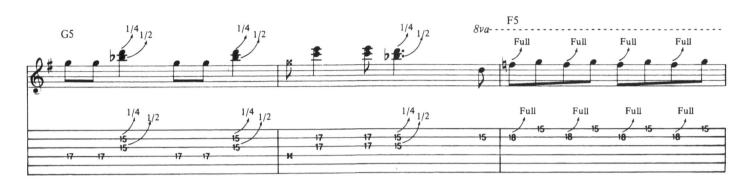

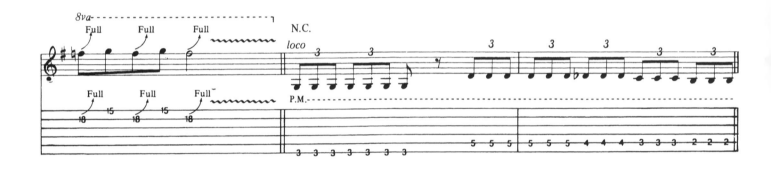

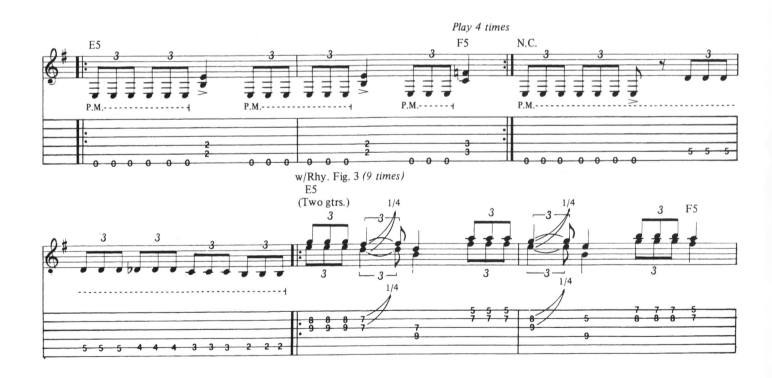

Paranoid

Words and Music by Anthony Iommi, John Osbourne, William Ward and Terence Butler

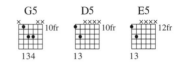

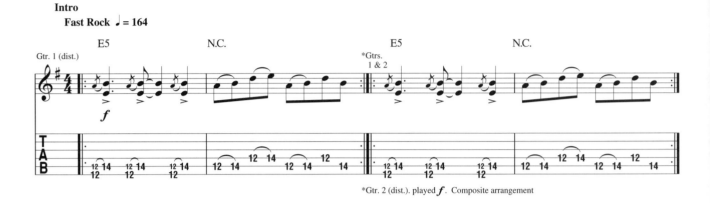

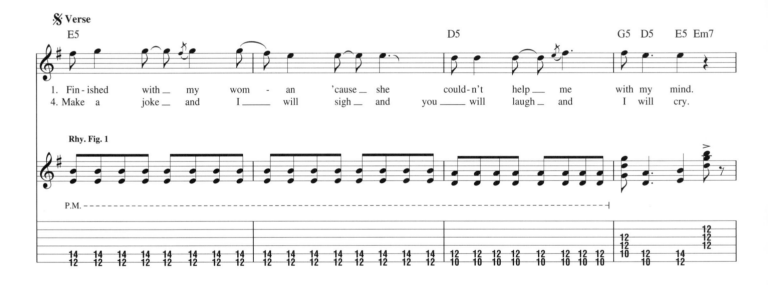

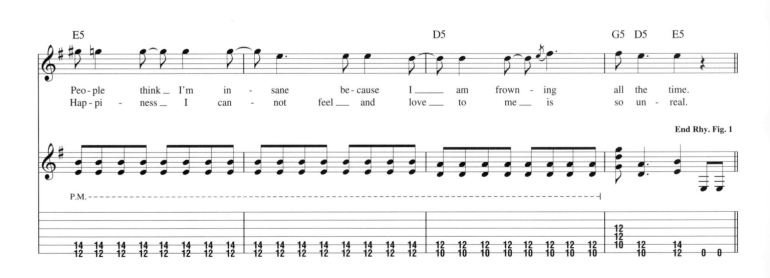

Interlude

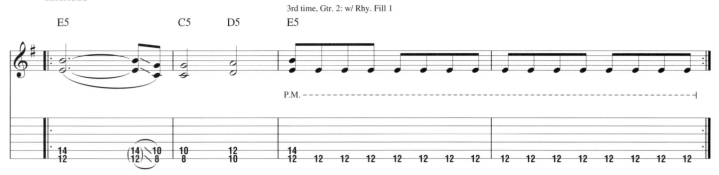

Verse

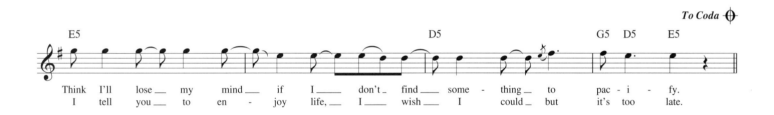

Bridge

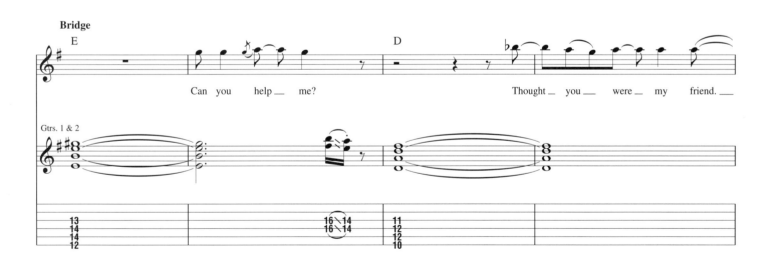

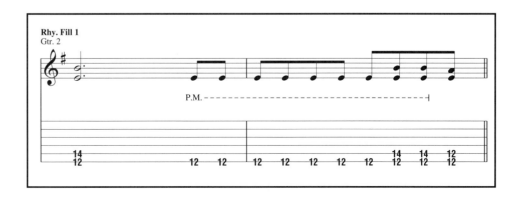

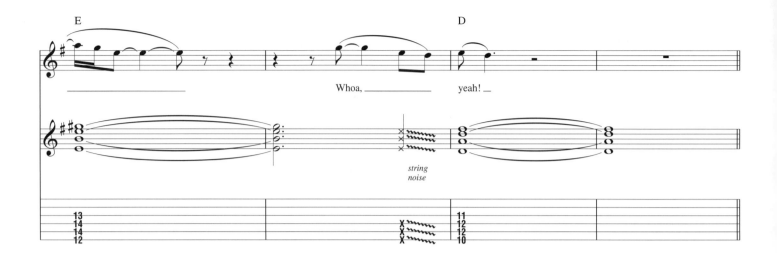

Whoa, _____ yeah! __

Interlude

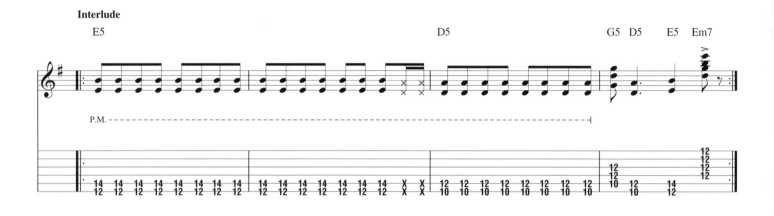

Verse

Gtrs. 1 & 2: w/ Rhy. Fig. 1

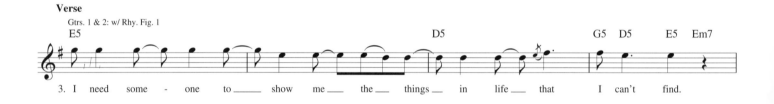

3. I need some - one to _____ show me __ the __ things __ in life __ that I can't find.

I can't see __ the things __ that make __ true hap - pi - ness, __ I must be blind.

Guitar Solo

Gtrs. 1 & 2: w/ Rhy. Fig. 1 (1st 4 meas., 4 times)

*Gtr. 3 (dist.)

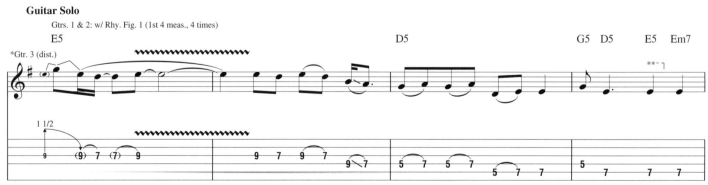

*With heavily distorted ring modulation effect in right channel.

**Played ahead
of the beat.

124

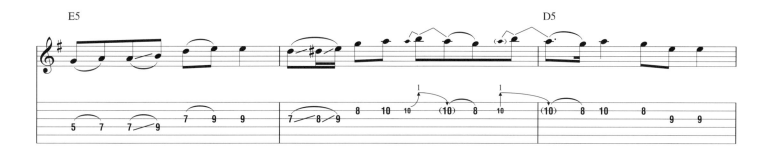

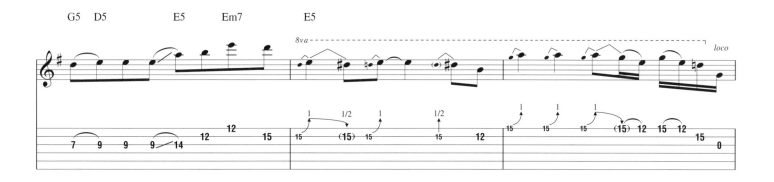

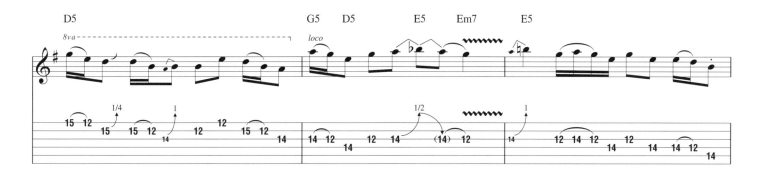

Interlude

D.S. al Coda

Gtrs. 1 & 2: w/ Rhy. Fig. 1 (1st 4 meas., 2 times)
Gtr. 3 tacet

Coda

Outro

Gtrs. 1 & 2: w/ Rhy. Fig. 1 (1st 7 meas.)

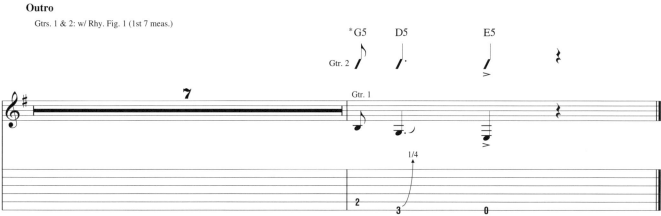

*See top of first page of song for chord diagrams pertaining to rhythm slashes.

Pride And Joy

Written by Stevie Ray Vaughan

Verse

1. Well, you've heard a-bout lov-in' giv-in' sight __ to the blind. __

* Mute w/ palm of pick hand.

My ba-by's lov-in' 'cause the sun __ to shine. __ An' she's my sweet __ lit-tle thang, __

she('s) my pride and joy. __ She('s) __ my

sweet lit-tle ba - by, I'm __ her __ lit-tle lov - er boy. __

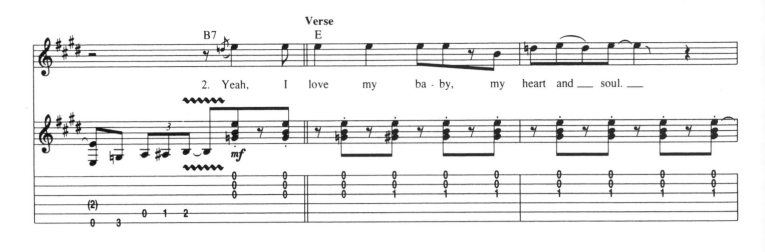

2. Yeah, I love my ba - by, my heart and __ soul. __

Love like ours __ ah, won't nev - er grow __ old. She('s) my sweet __ lit - tle thang, __

she('s) my pride and joy. __ She('s) __ my

sweet lit - tle ba - by, I'm __ her lit - tle lov - er boy.

3. Yeah, I love my la-dy to be long and __ lean. __

You mess with her, you'll see a man get-tin' mean. __ She('s) my sweet __ lit-tle thang, __

she('s) my pride and joy. __ She('s) my

sweet _ lit-tle ba - by, I'm __ her __ lit - tle lov - er boy. __

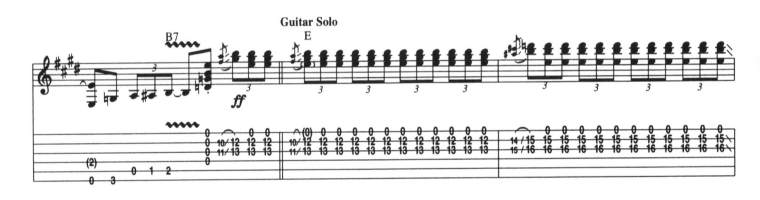

Guitar Solo

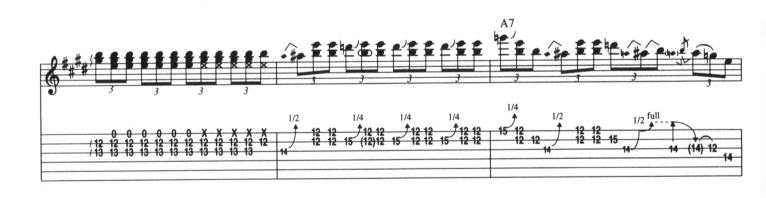

The Number Of The Beast

Words and Music by Steven Harris

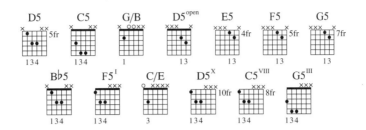

> *Spoken:* *Woe to you, oh, Earth and Sea,*
> *For the Devil sends the beast with wrath,*
> *Because he knows the time is short...*
> *Let him who hath understanding*
> *Reckon the number of the beast,*
> *For it is a human number.*
> *Its number is six hundred and sixty six.*
>
> *- Revelations Ch. 13 v. 8*

Intro
Fast Rock ♩ = 195

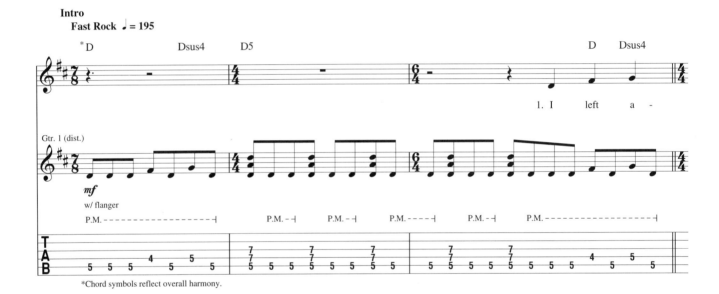

*Chord symbols reflect overall harmony.

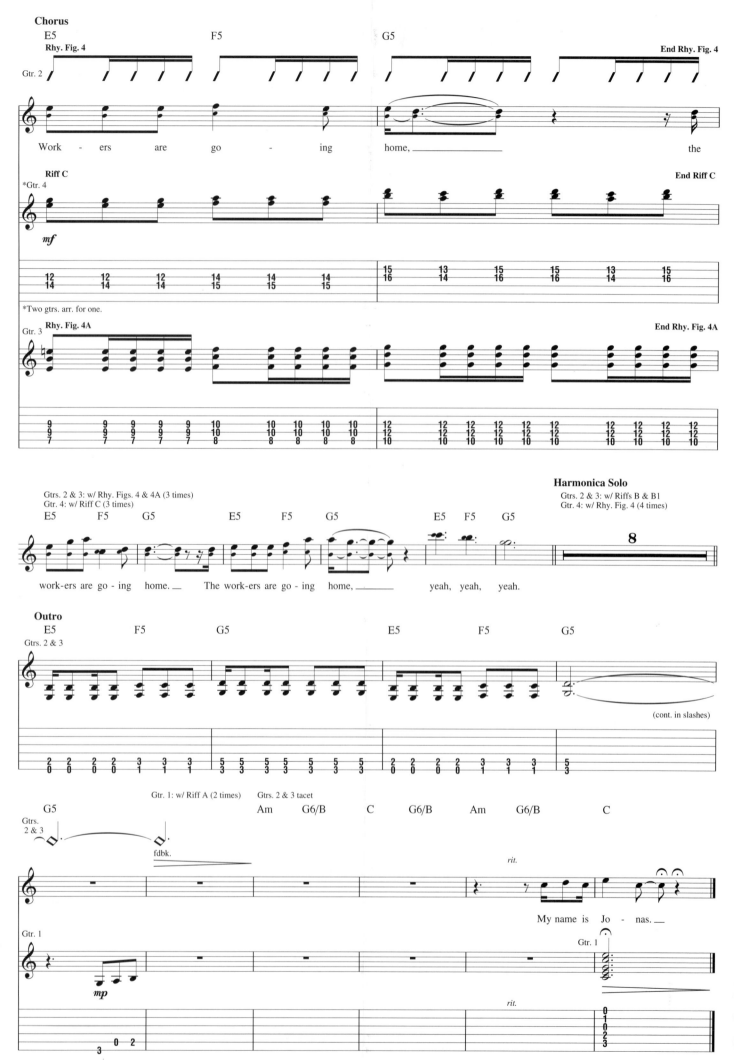

4. Well, I love my ba-by like the fin-est w, wine. _

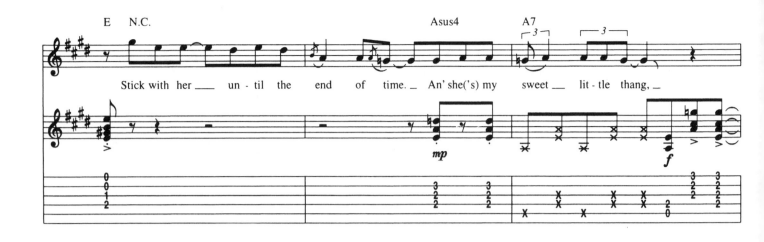

Stick with her ___ un - til the end of time. ___ An' she('s) my ___ sweet ___ lit - tle thang, ___

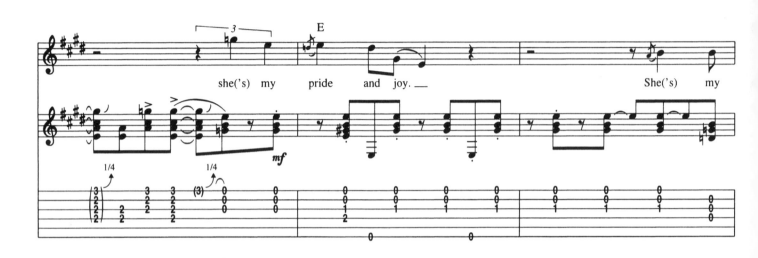

she('s) my pride and joy. ___ She('s) my

sweet lit - tle ba - by, I'm ___ her ___ lit - tle lov - er boy.

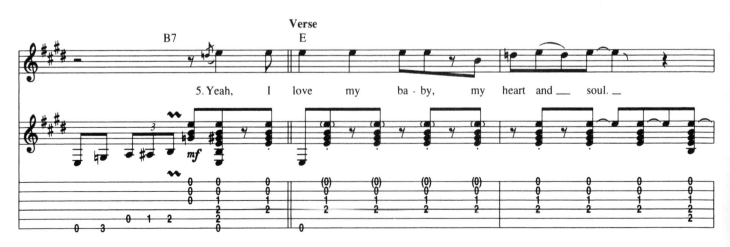

Verse

5. Yeah, I love my ba - by, my heart and ___ soul.

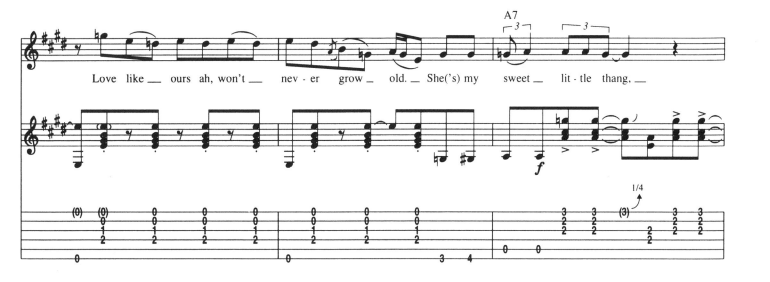

Love like ___ ours ah, won't ___ nev - er grow ___ old. She('s) my sweet ___ lit - tle thang, ___

she('s) my pride and joy. ___ She('s) ___ my

sweet lit-tle ba - by, I'm ___ her ___ lit - tle lov - er boy. ___

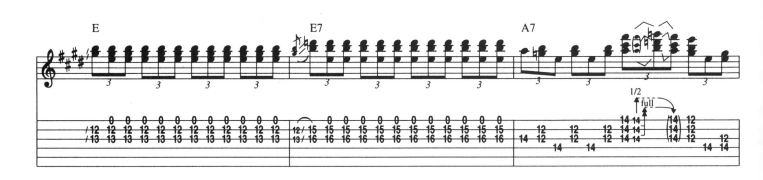

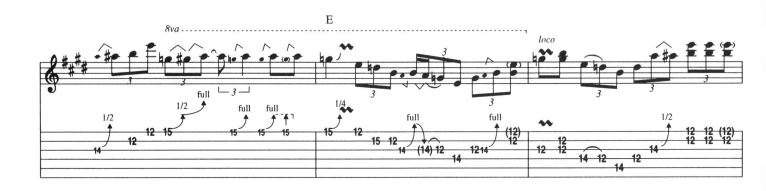

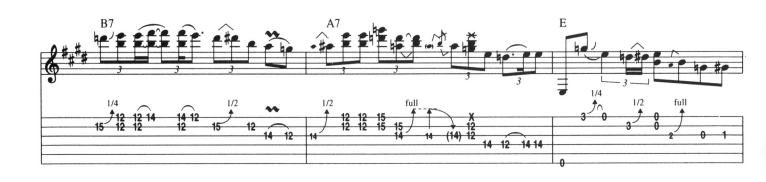

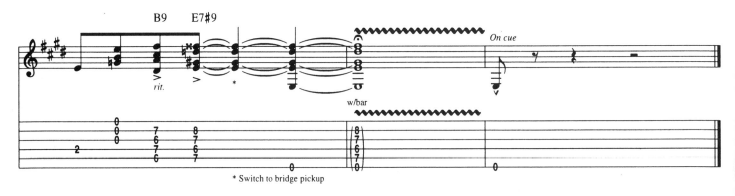

* Switch to bridge pickup

Raining Blood

Words and Music by Jeff Hanneman and Kerry King

Tune down 1/2 step:
(low to high) Eb-Ab-Db-Gb-Bb-Eb

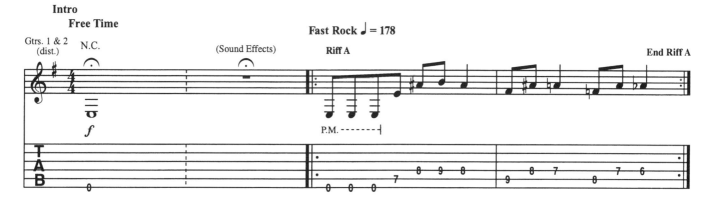

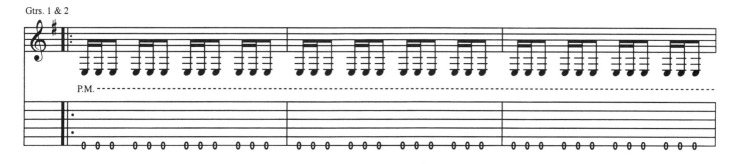

136

Outro
Faster ♩ = 247
Double-time Feel

Gtrs. 3 & 4 (dist.): w/ misc. bar effects

Play 4 times

P.M. throughout

Play 9 times

Gtrs. 1, 2, 3 & 4 tacet

(Sound Effects)

Rock And Roll All Nite

Words and Music by Paul Stanley and Gene Simmons

Tune Down 1/2 Step
①= Eb ④= Db
②= Bb ⑤= Ab
③= Gb ⑥= Eb

Intro

Anthem Rock ♩ = 138

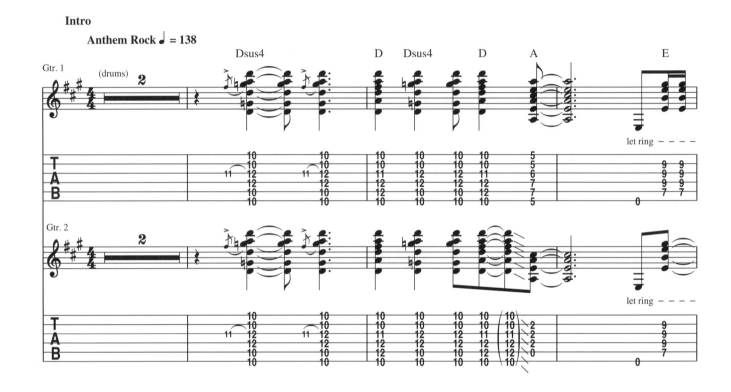

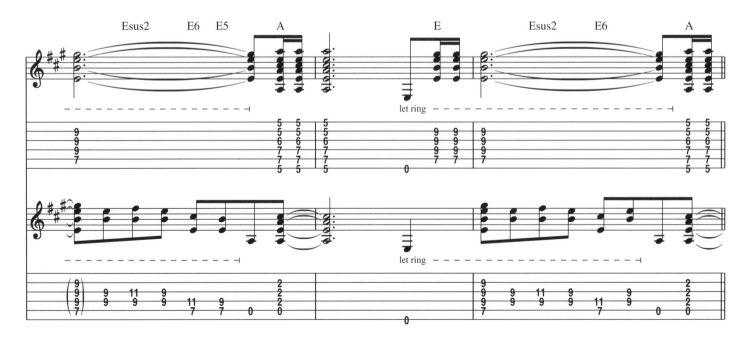

Verse

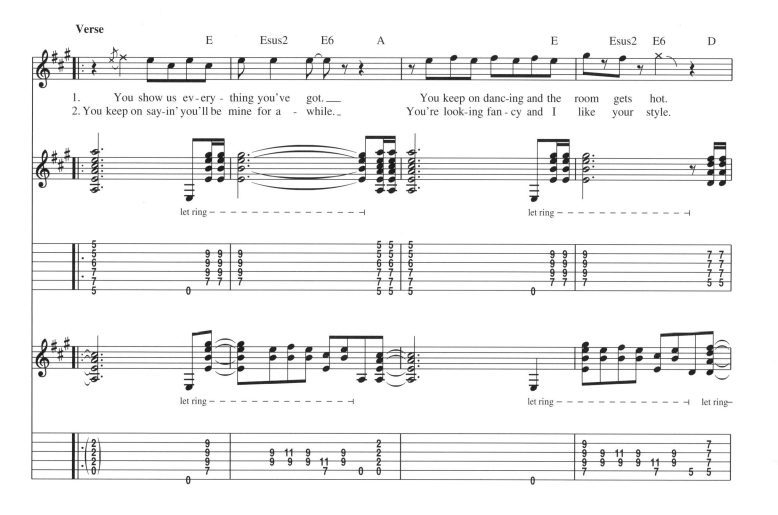

1. You show us ev-ery-thing you've got. ___ You keep on danc-ing and the room gets hot.
2. You keep on say-in' you'll be mine for a - while. ___ You're look-ing fan-cy and I like your style.

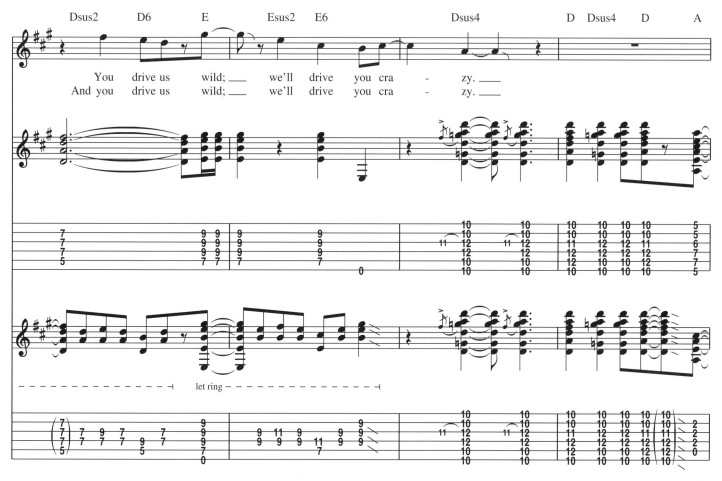

You drive us wild; ___ we'll drive you cra - zy. ___
And you drive us wild; ___ we'll drive you cra - zy.

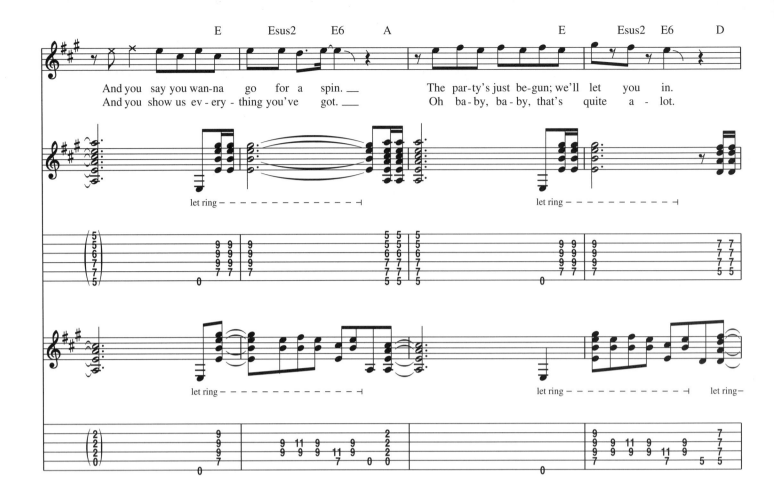

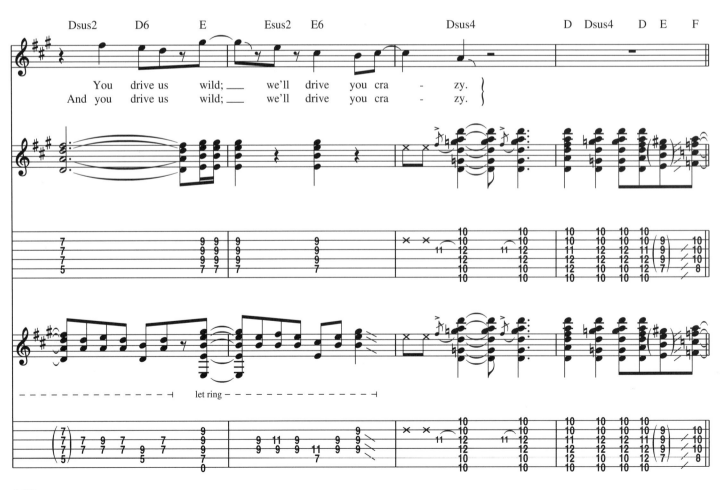

142

Pre-Chorus

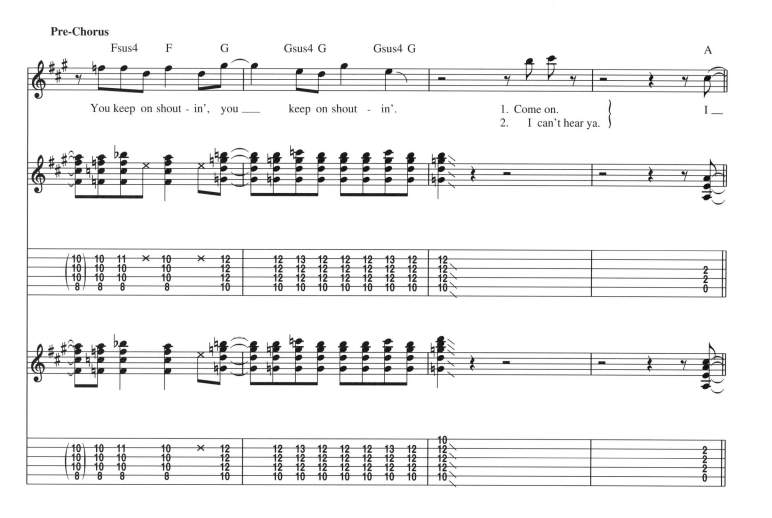

You keep on shout-in', you ___ keep on shout-in'. 1. Come on. I ___

2. I can't hear ya.

Chorus

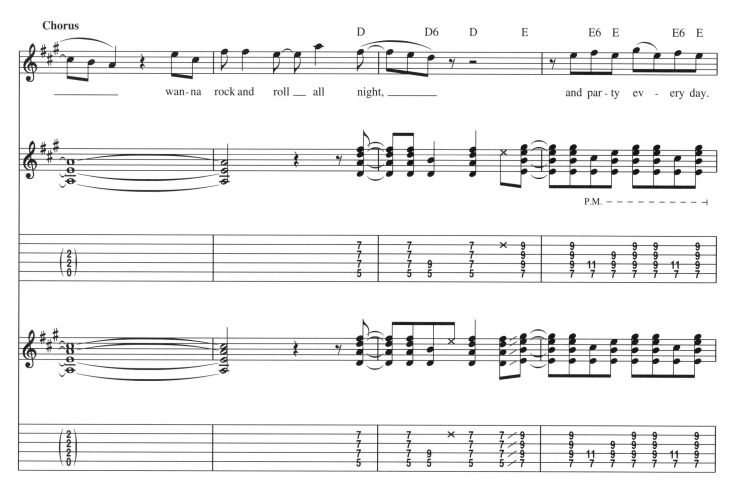

___ wan-na rock and roll ___ all night, ___ and par-ty ev - ery day.

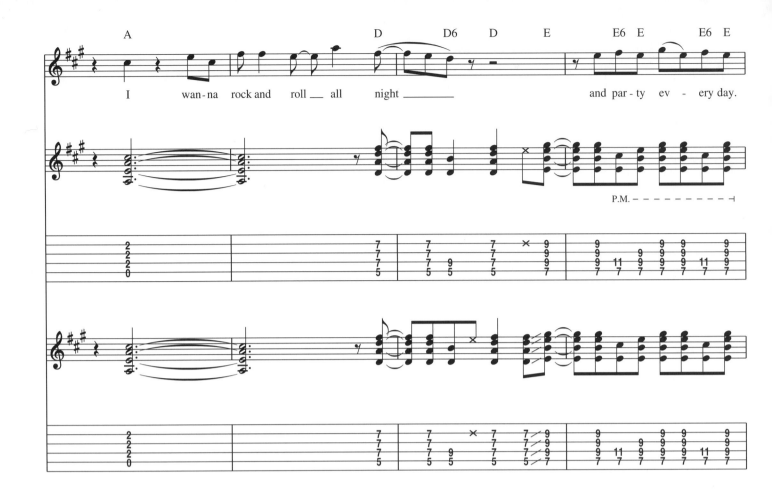

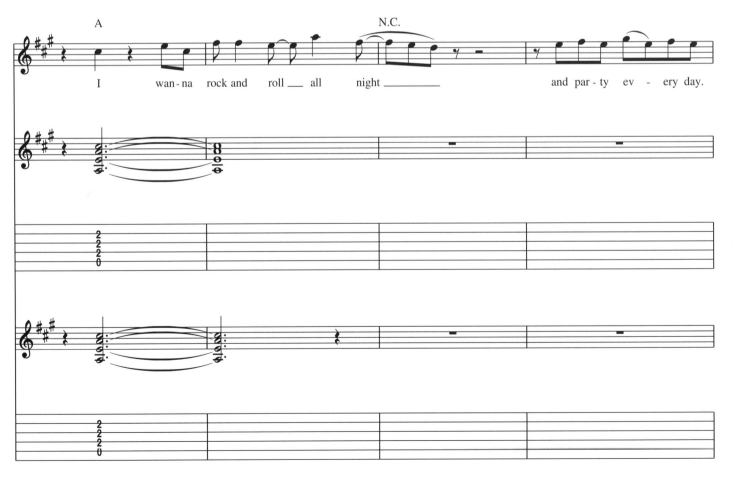

144

I wan-na rock and roll __ all night _____ and par-ty ev - ery day.

You keep on shout-in'. You ___ keep on shout - in'.

What?

I ___

146

Chorus

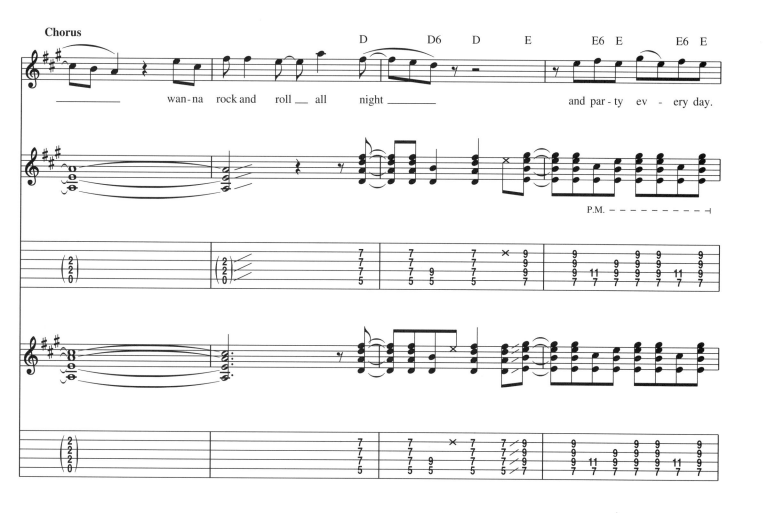

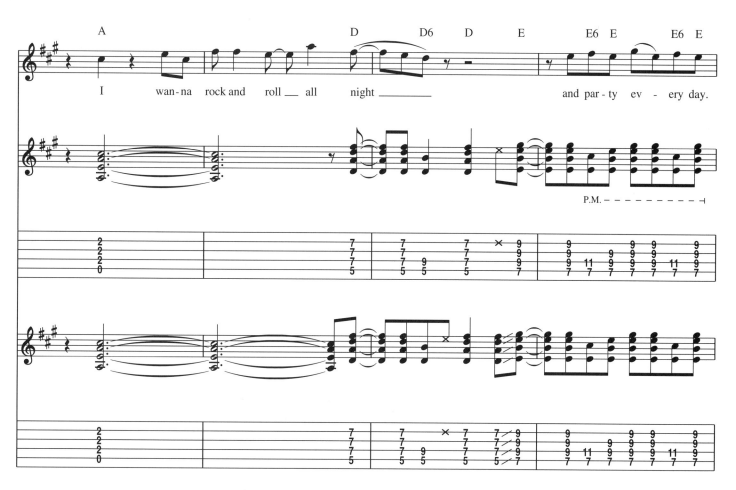

147

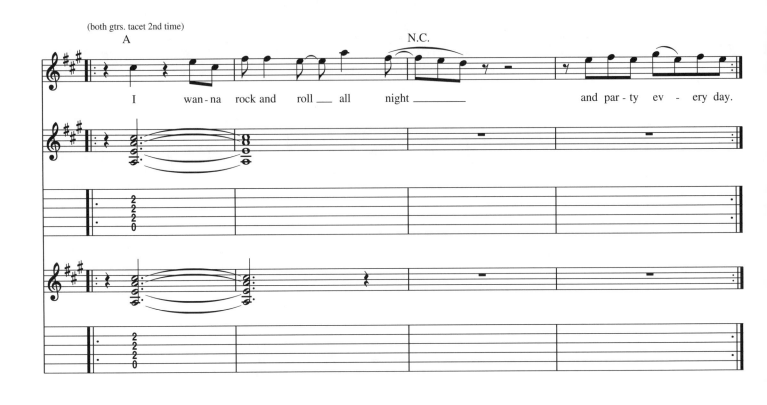

(both gtrs. tacet 2nd time)

I wan-na rock and roll __ all night _____ and par - ty ev - er - y day.

Outro

Rock You Like A Hurricane

Words and Music by Herman Rarebell, Klaus Meine and Rudolf Schenker

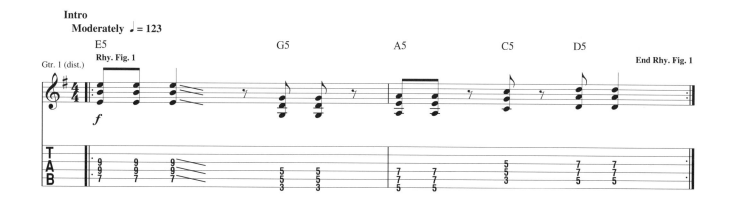

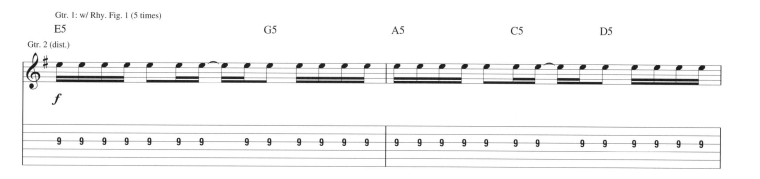

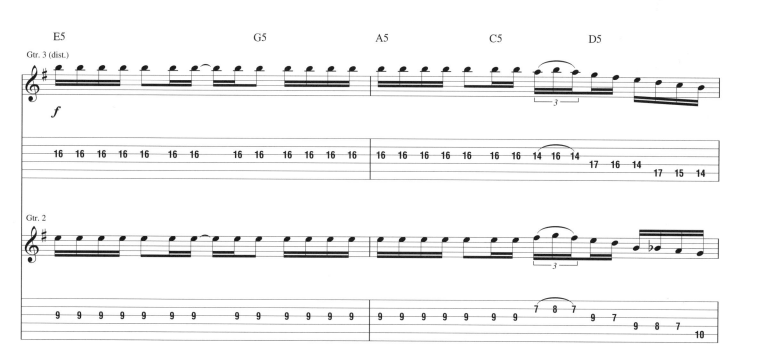

night was shak - ing and pret - ty loud. ___ My

cat is purr - ing, it scratch - es my skin. ___ So,

what is wrong ___ with an - oth - er sin? ___ The bitch is hun - gry, she

needs to tell, ___ so give her inch - es and feed her well. ___ More

days to come, ___ new plac - es to go. ___ I've got to leave, ___ it's

157

Sabotage

Words and Music by Michael Diamond, Adam Yauch and Adam Horovitz

Ab5

Intro
Moderately slow ♩ = 84

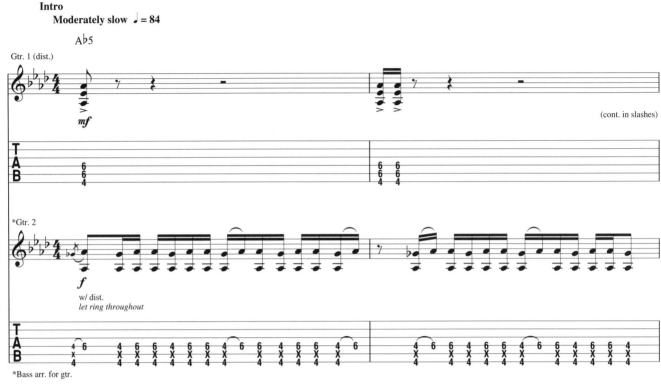

*Bass arr. for gtr.

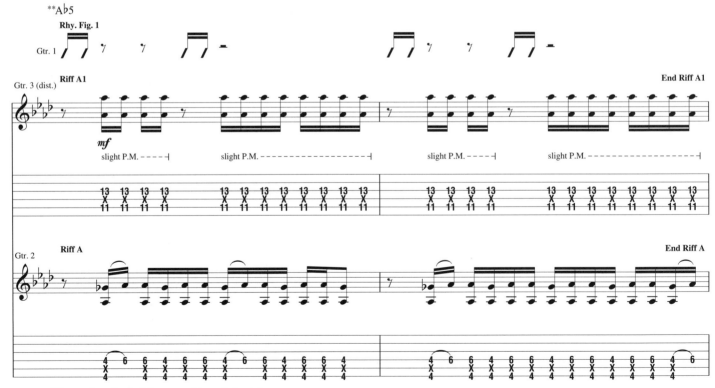

**See top of page for chord diagram pertaining to rhythm slashes.

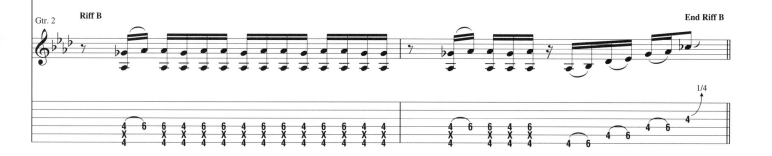

%. Verse

Gtrs. 2 & 3: w/ Riffs A & A1 (4 times)
1st time, Gtr. 4: w/ Fill 1 (4 times)

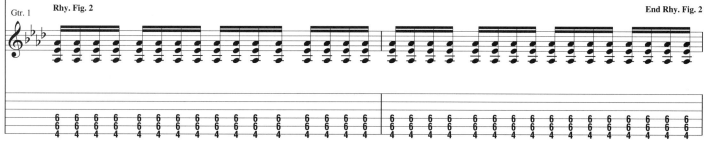

159

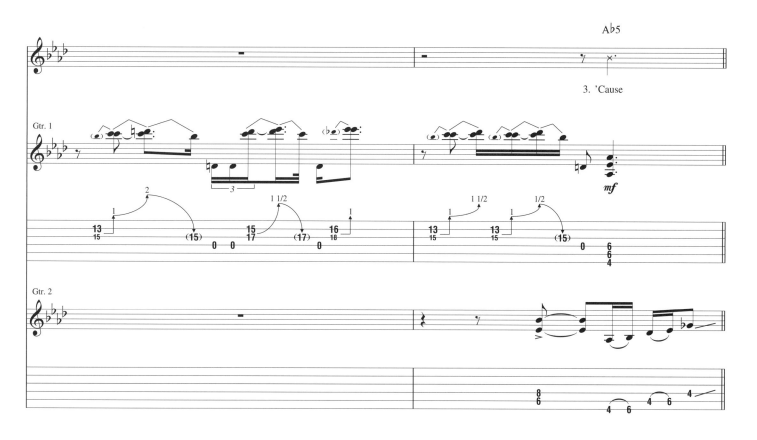

Verse

Gtr. 1: w/ Rhy. Fig. 2 (2 times)
Gtrs. 2 & 3: w/ Riffs A & A1 (2 times)

A♭5

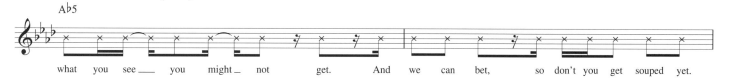

what you see ___ you might ___ not get. And we can bet, so don't you get souped yet.

Gtr. 4: w/ Fill 2

Schem-in' on a thing that's a mi-rage. ___ I'm try-in' to tell you now it's sab - o - tage. ___

Turntable Solo

Gtr. 1: w/ Rhy. Fig. 1
Gtrs. 2 & 3: w/ Riffs A & A1 (1 1/2 times)

Gtr. 3 tacet

A♭5

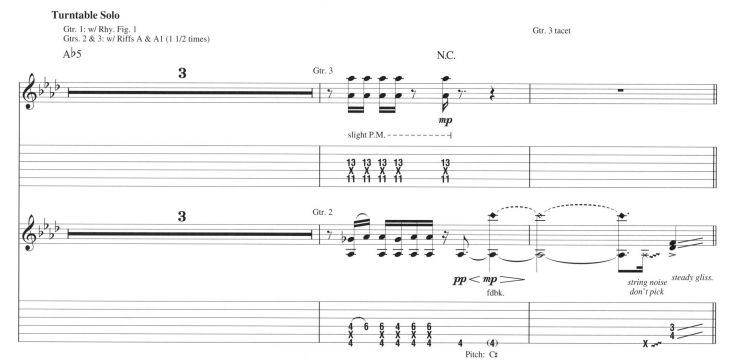

Bass Solo

Gtr. 2

N.C.

Why? —
(Why? —

Bridge

Gtr. 1: w/ Rhy. Fig. 2 (4 times)
Gtr. 3: w/ Riff A1 (4 times)

A♭5

Our

backs are now a - gainst the wall. _____

Interlude

Gtr. 1: w/ Rhy. Fig. 1 (2 times)
Gtr. 3: w/ Riff A1 (2 times)

Ab5

*Spoken: Lis - ten all, y'all, __ it's a sab - o - tage. __   Lis - ten all, y'all, __ it's a sab - o - tage. __

*p < f, next 4 meas.

D.S. al Coda

Lis - ten all, y'all, __ it's a sab - o - tage. __   Lis - ten all, y'all, __ it's a sab - o - tage. __

4. *Spoken:* I

Coda

Outro

Ab5

Gtr. 1

Gtr. 3

(sampled fdbk.)

slight P.M. - - - - - - - -|

Gtr. 2

Same Old Song And Dance

Words and Music by Steven Tyler and Joe Perry

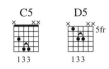

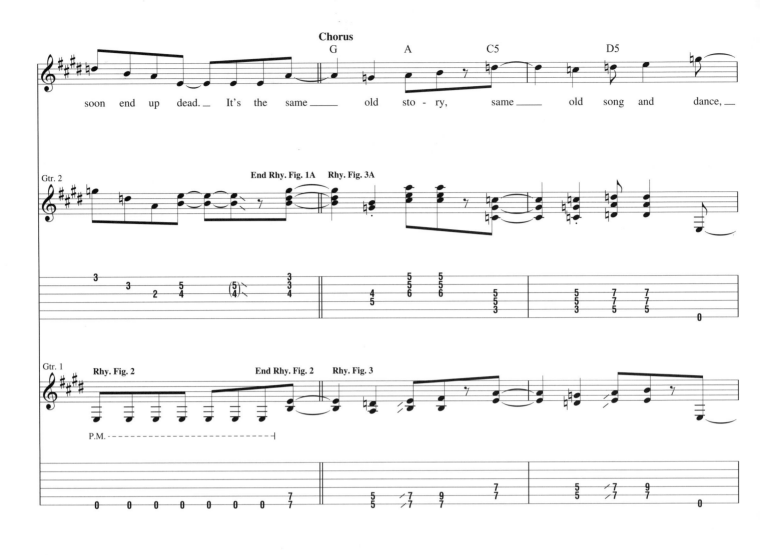

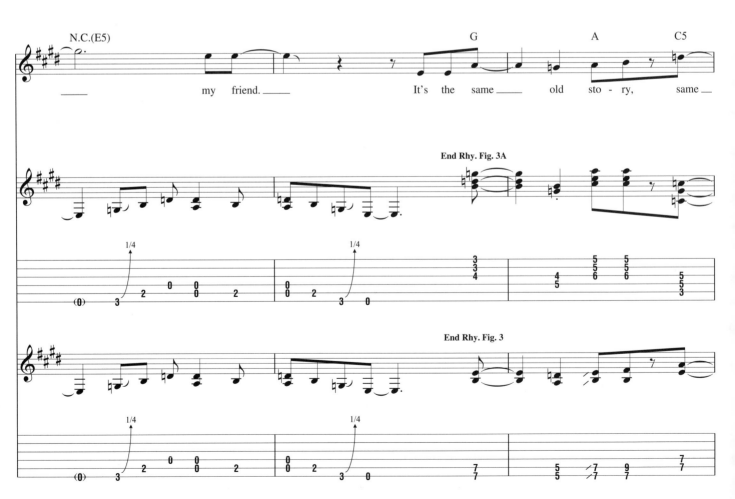

166

but you ain't gon- na find it a-round. It's the same ___ old sto- ry, same ___

___ old song and dance, ___ my friend. ___ It's the same ___

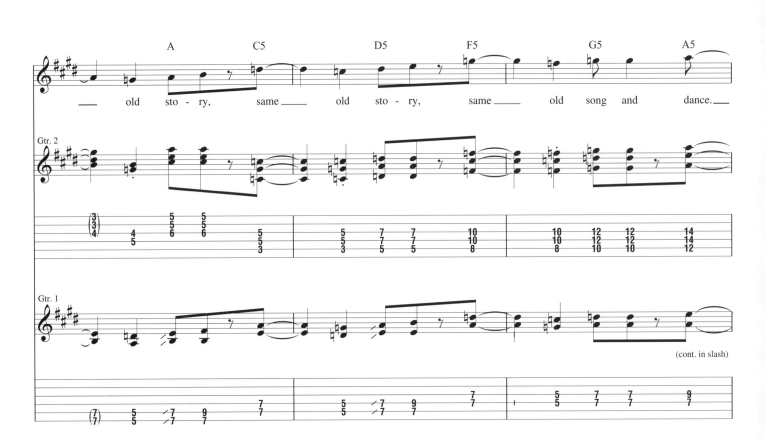

___ old sto- ry, same ___ old sto- ry, same ___ old song and dance.___

(cont. in slash)

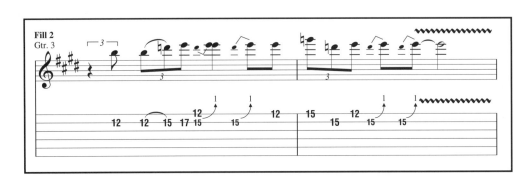

Fill 2
Gtr. 3

Fill 4
Gtr. 3

time con - nec - tion, change___ your di - rec - tion. You ain't___ gon - na change it, can't___

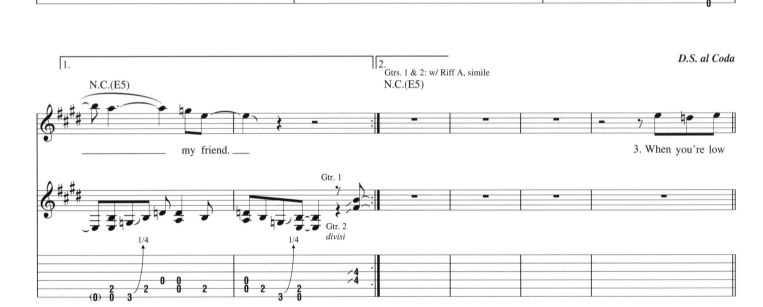

re - ar - range it. Can't___ stand the pain when it's all___ the same___ to you___

D.S. al Coda

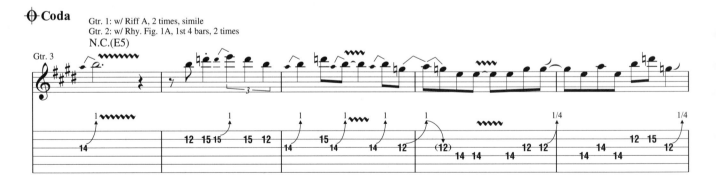

_____ my friend. ___

3. When you're low

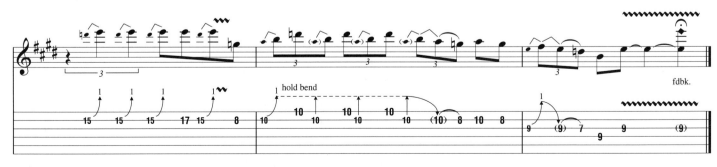

School's Out

Words and Music by Alice Cooper and Michael Bruce

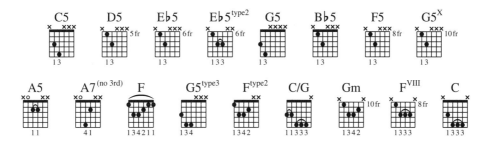

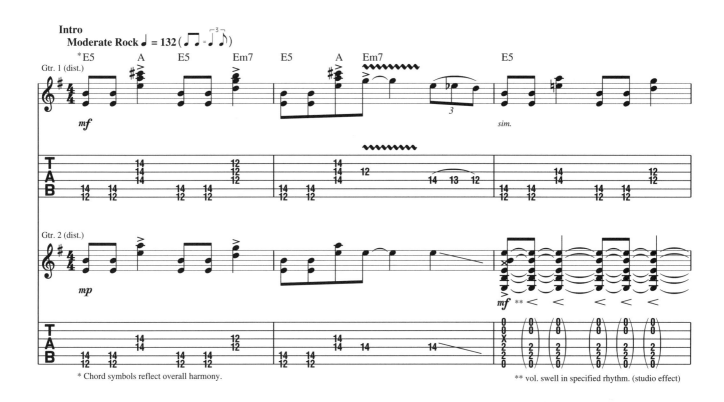

* Chord symbols reflect overall harmony.

** vol. swell in specified rhythm. (studio effect)

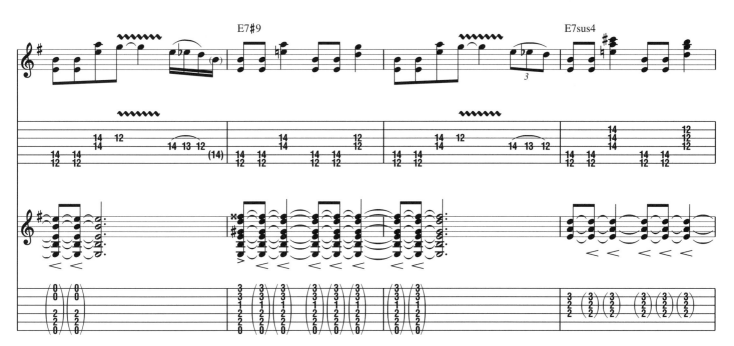

Verse

Gtr. 2: w/ Rhy. Fig. 2, 4 times

1. Well, we got _____ no _____ choice, _____ all the girls _____

Gtr. 1: w/ Rhy. Fig. 3, 3 times

_____ and boys _____ mak- in' all _____ their noise, _____

_____ 'cause they found _____ new _____ toys. _____ Well, we

Pre-Chorus

can't sa - lute __ ya, can't find a flag. __ If that don't suit ya, that's a drag. __

Chorus

School's out for sum-mer!

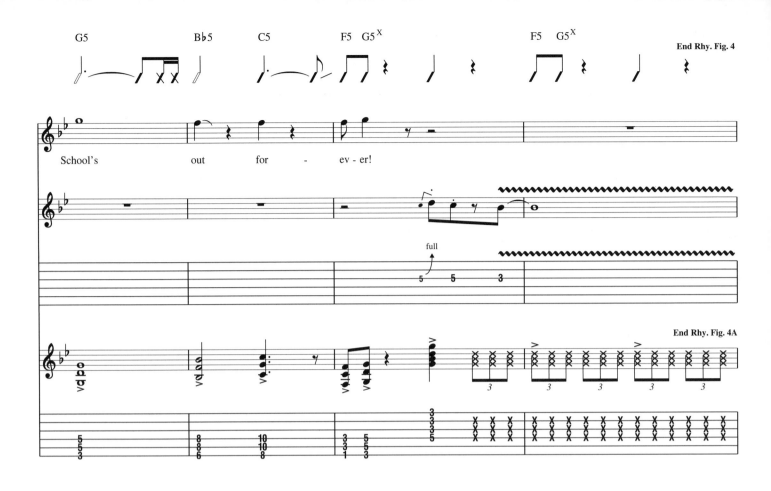

School's out for - ev - er!

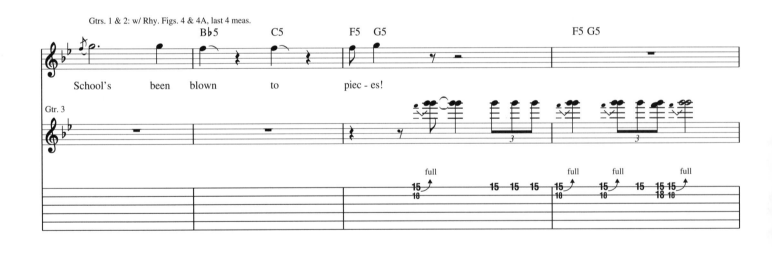

Gtrs. 1 & 2: w/ Rhy. Figs. 4 & 4A, last 4 meas.

School's been blown to piec - es!

Gtr. 3

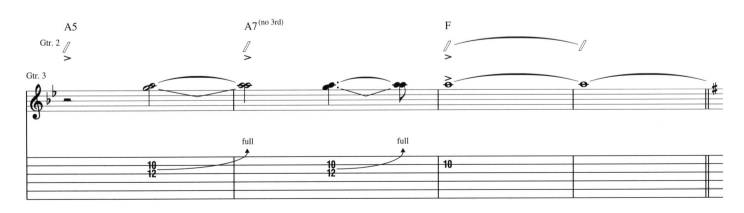

Bridge

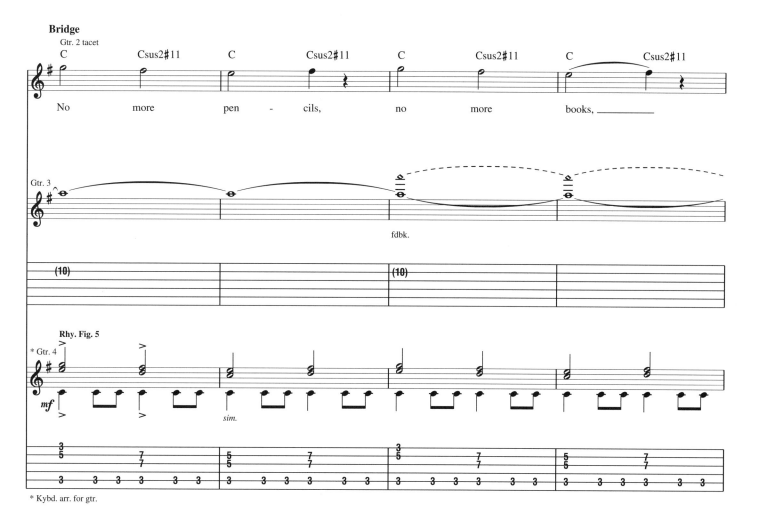

* Kybd. arr. for gtr.

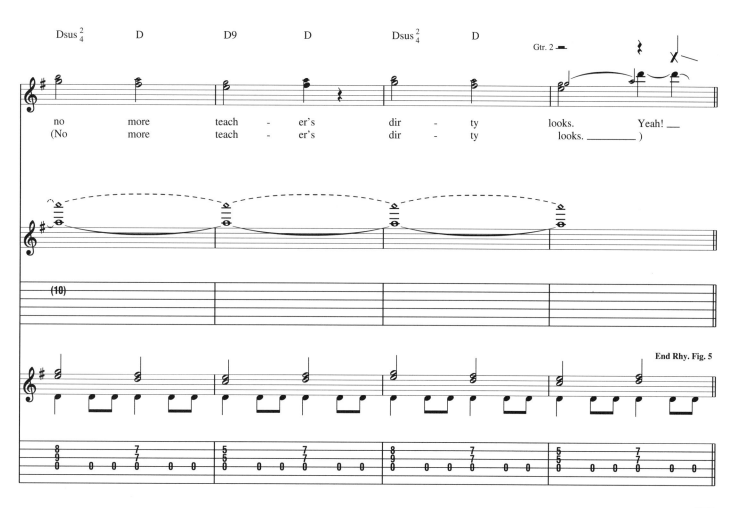

The Seeker

Words and Music by Pete Townshend

Story Of My Life

Words and Music by Michael Ness

Suck My Kiss

Words and Music by Anthony Kiedis, Flea, John Frusciante and Chad Smith

I am ___ what I am, ___ most moth-er-fuck-ers don't give a damn. ___ Oh, ba - by, think you can?
I need ___ re - lief, ___ do you want me girl to be your thief? ___ Oh, ba - by, just for you I'd

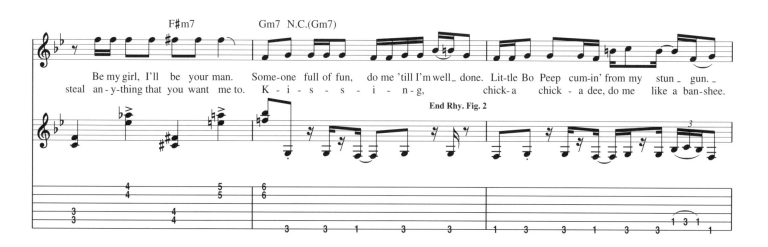

Be my girl, I'll be your man. Some-one full of fun, do me 'till I'm well_ done. Lit-tle Bo Peep cum-in' from my stun _ gun. _
steal an - y-thing that you want me to. K - i - s - s - i - n - g, chick-a chick - a dee, do me like a ban-shee.

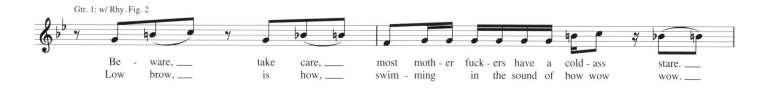

Be - ware, ___ take care, ___ most moth - er fuck - ers have a cold - ass stare. ___
Low brow, ___ is how, ___ swim - ming in the sound of bow wow wow. ___

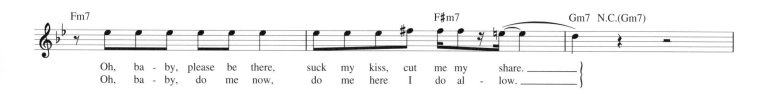

Oh, ba - by, please be there, suck my kiss, cut me my share. _____
Oh, ba - by, do me now, do me here I do al - low. _____

Hit me! You can't hurt me! _ Suck my kiss! Kiss me! Please per - vert me!

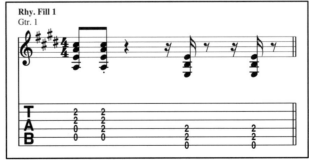

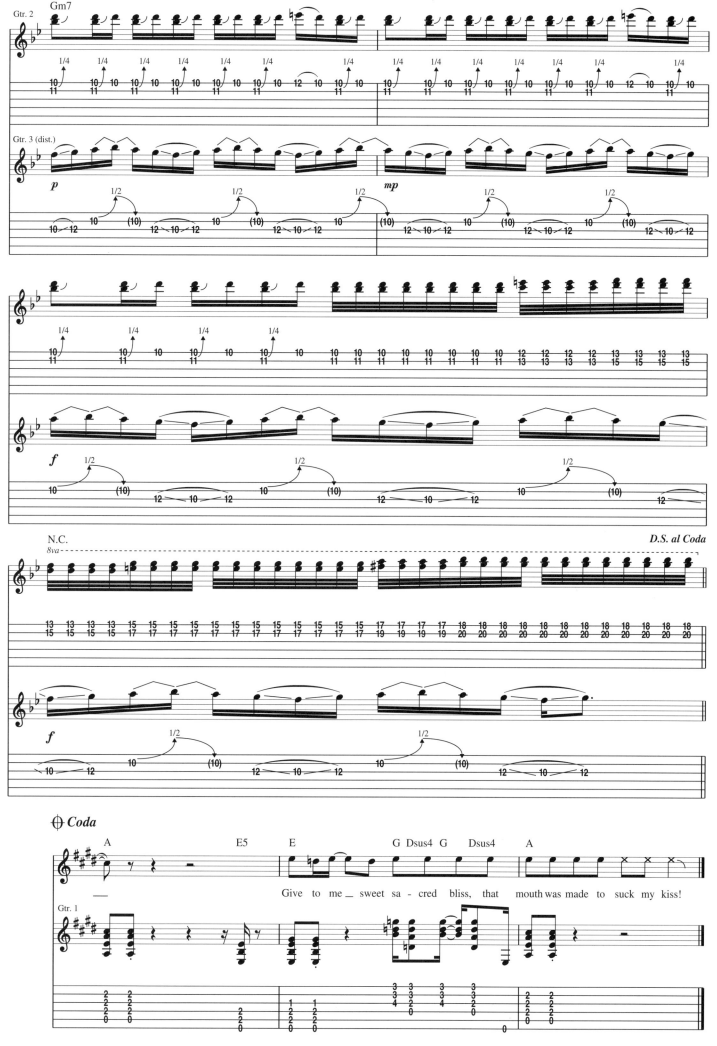

Sunshine Of Your Love

Words and Music by Jack Bruce, Pete Brown and Eric Clapton

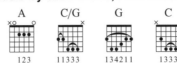

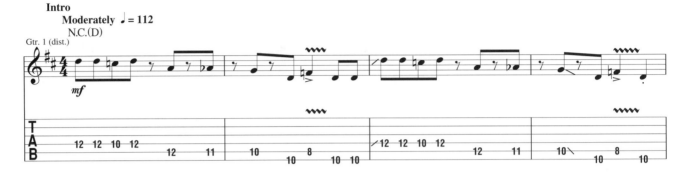

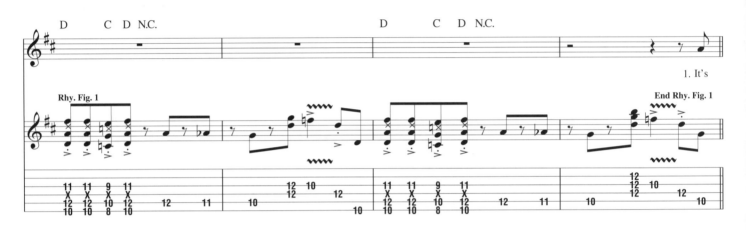

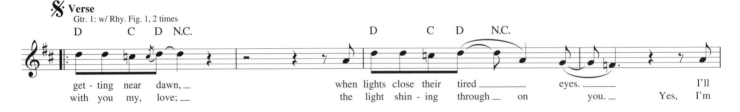

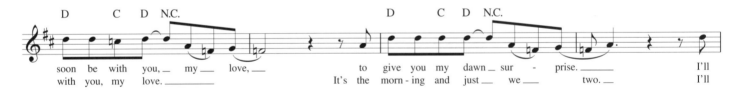

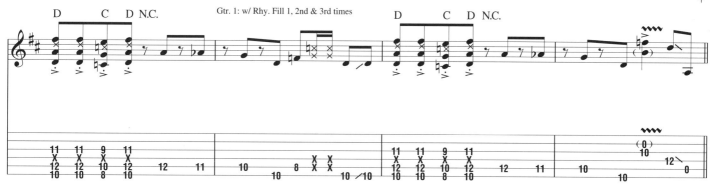

Chorus

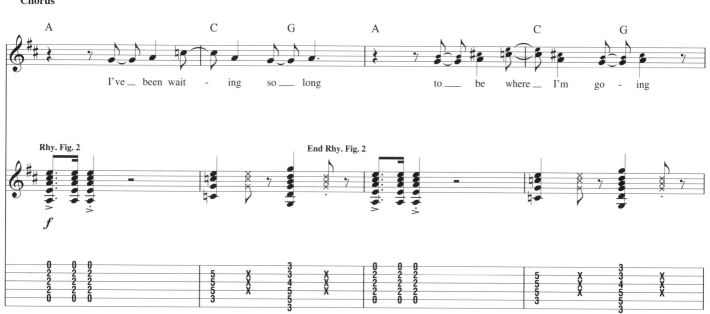

I've __ been wait - ing so __ long to __ be where __ I'm go - ing

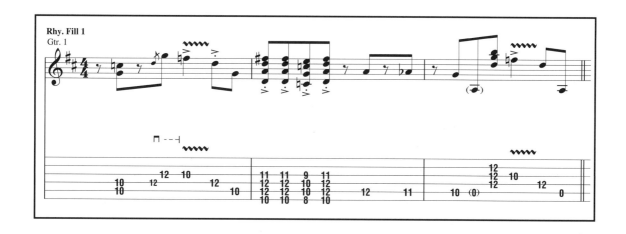

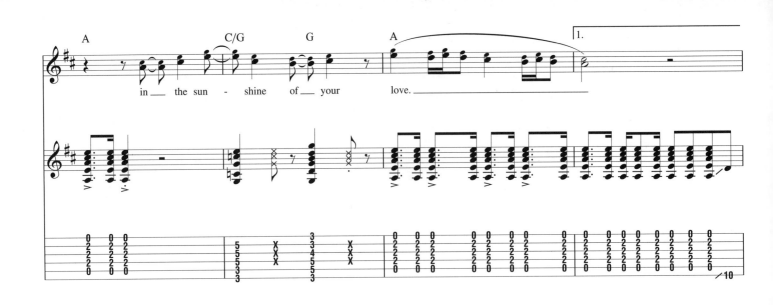

in ___ the sun - shine of ___ your love. ____

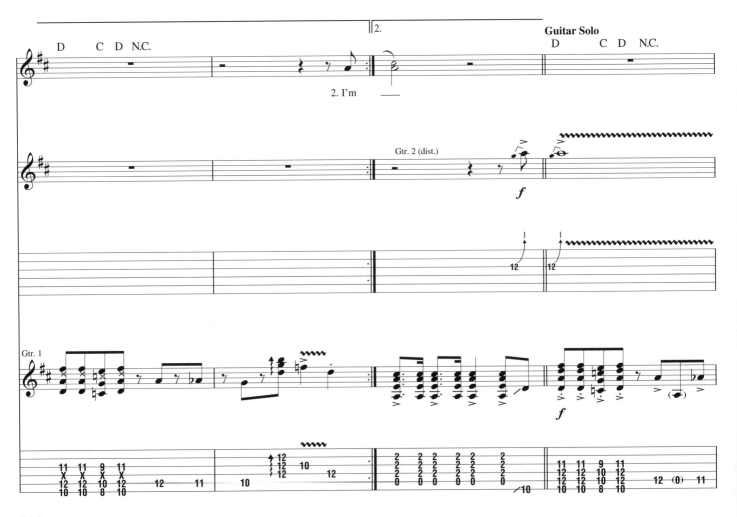

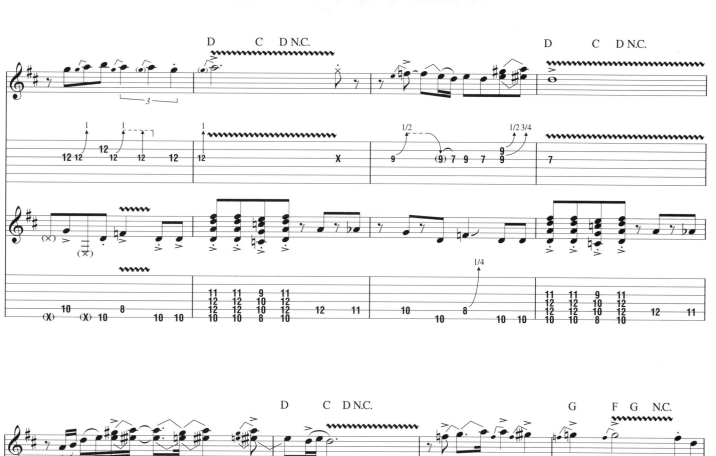

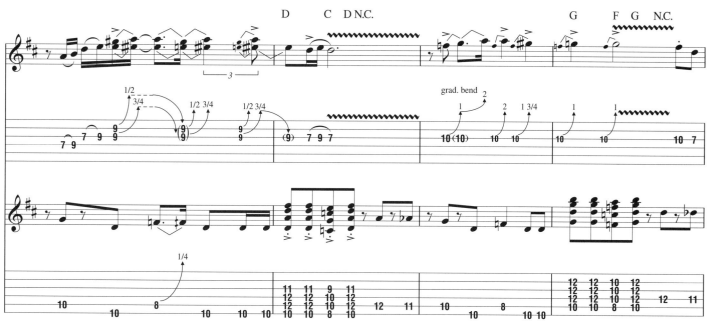

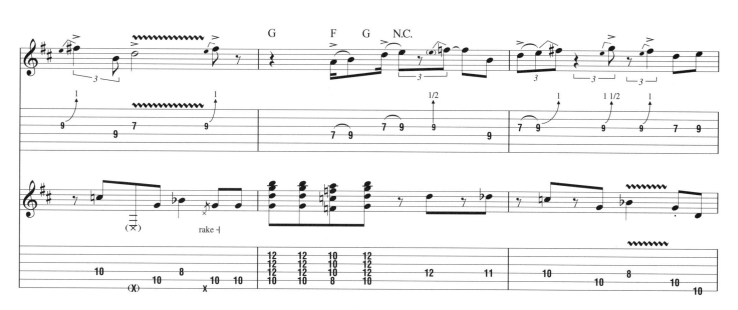

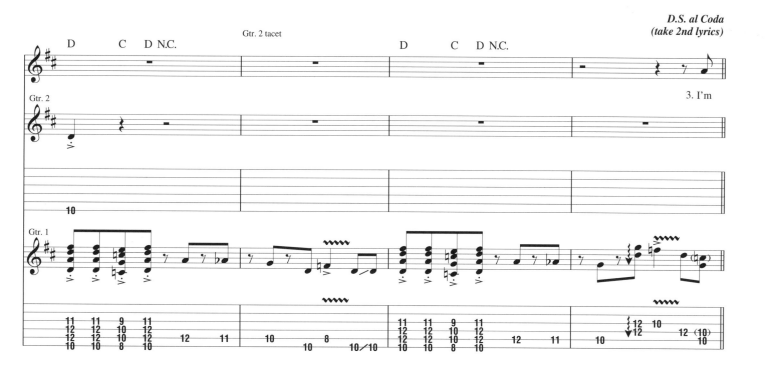

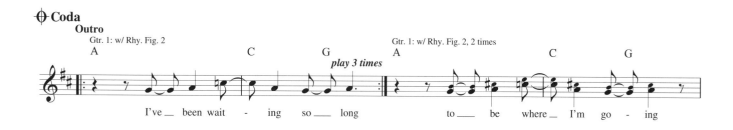

I've __ been wait - ing so __ long   to __ be where __ I'm go - ing

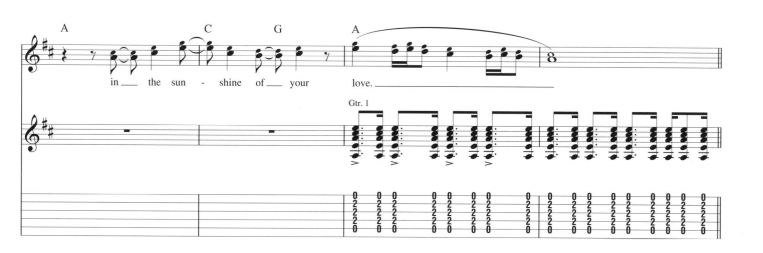

in __ the sun - shine of __ your   love. __

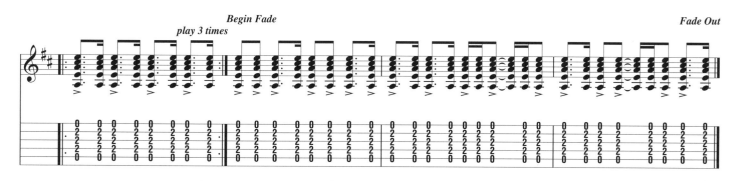

When You Were Young

Words and Music by Brandon Flowers, Dave Keuning, Mark Stoermer and Ronnie Vannucci

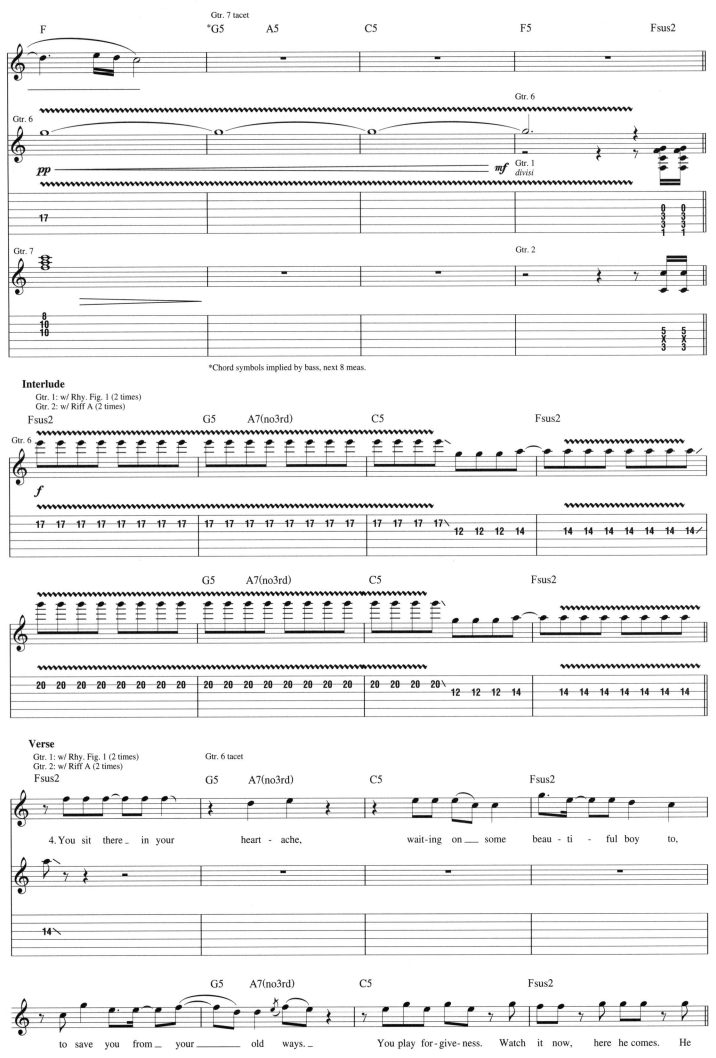

*Chord symbols implied by bass, next 8 meas.

Interlude

Verse

Guitar Notation Legend

Guitar music can be notated three different ways: on a *musical staff*, in *tablature*, and in *rhythm slashes*.

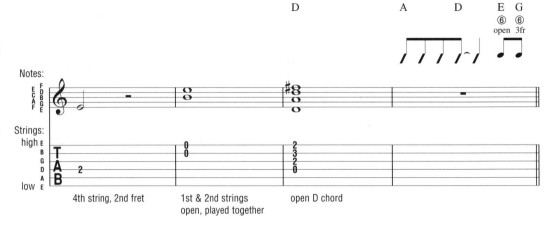

RHYTHM SLASHES are written above the staff. Strum chords in the rhythm indicated. Use the chord diagrams found at the top of the first page of the transcription for the appropriate chord voicings. Round noteheads indicate single notes.

THE MUSICAL STAFF shows pitches and rhythms and is divided by bar lines into measures. Pitches are named after the first seven letters of the alphabet.

TABLATURE graphically represents the guitar fingerboard. Each horizontal line represents a string, and each number represents a fret.

Definitions for Special Guitar Notation

HALF-STEP BEND: Strike the note and bend up 1/2 step.

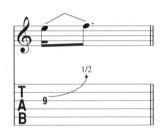

WHOLE-STEP BEND: Strike the note and bend up one step.

GRACE NOTE BEND: Strike the note and immediately bend up as indicated.

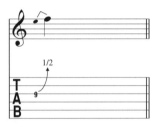

SLIGHT (MICROTONE) BEND: Strike the note and bend up 1/4 step.

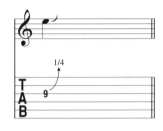

BEND AND RELEASE: Strike the note and bend up as indicated, then release back to the original note. Only the first note is struck.

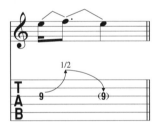

PRE-BEND: Bend the note as indicated, then strike it.

PRE-BEND AND RELEASE: Bend the note as indicated. Strike it and release the bend back to the original note.

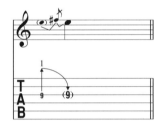

UNISON BEND: Strike the two notes simultaneously and bend the lower note up to the pitch of the higher.

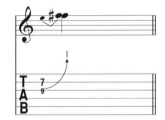

VIBRATO: The string is vibrated by rapidly bending and releasing the note with the fretting hand.

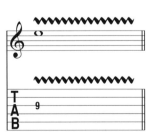

WIDE VIBRATO: The pitch is varied to a greater degree by vibrating with the fretting hand.

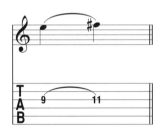

HAMMER-ON: Strike the first (lower) note with one finger, then sound the higher note (on the same string) with another finger by fretting it without picking.

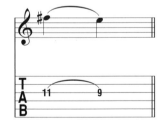

PULL-OFF: Place both fingers on the notes to be sounded. Strike the first note and without picking, pull the finger off to sound the second (lower) note.

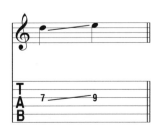

LEGATO SLIDE: Strike the first note and then slide the same fret-hand finger up or down to the second note. The second note is not struck.

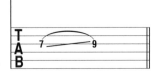

SHIFT SLIDE: Same as legato slide, except the second note is struck.

TRILL: Very rapidly alternate between the notes indicated by continuously hammering on and pulling off.

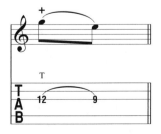

TAPPING: Hammer ("tap") the fret indicated with the pick-hand index or middle finger and pull off to the note fretted by the fret hand.

NATURAL HARMONIC: Strike the note while the fret-hand lightly touches the string directly over the fret indicated.

PINCH HARMONIC: The note is fretted normally and a harmonic is produced by adding the edge of the thumb or the tip of the index finger of the pick hand to the normal pick attack.

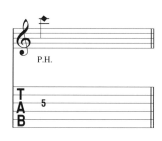

HARP HARMONIC: The note is fretted normally and a harmonic is produced by gently resting the pick hand's index finger directly above the indicated fret (in parentheses) while the pick hand's thumb or pick assists by plucking the appropriate string.

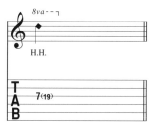

PICK SCRAPE: The edge of the pick is rubbed down (or up) the string, producing a scratchy sound.

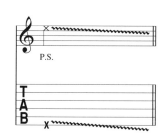

MUFFLED STRINGS: A percussive sound is produced by laying the fret hand across the string(s) without depressing, and striking them with the pick hand.

PALM MUTING: The note is partially muted by the pick hand lightly touching the string(s) just before the bridge.

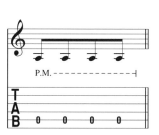

RAKE: Drag the pick across the strings indicated with a single motion.

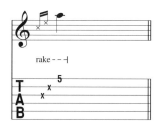

TREMOLO PICKING: The note is picked as rapidly and continuously as possible.

ARPEGGIATE: Play the notes of the chord indicated by quickly rolling them from bottom to top.

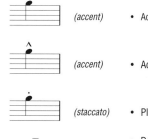

VIBRATO BAR DIVE AND RETURN: The pitch of the note or chord is dropped a specified number of steps (in rhythm), then returned to the original pitch.

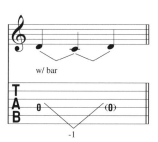

VIBRATO BAR SCOOP: Depress the bar just before striking the note, then quickly release the bar.

VIBRATO BAR DIP: Strike the note and then immediately drop a specified number of steps, then release back to the original pitch.

Additional Musical Definitions

> (accent)	• Accentuate note (play it louder).	
^ (accent)	• Accentuate note with great intensity.	
• (staccato)	• Play the note short.	
⊓	• Downstroke	
∨	• Upstroke	

Rhy. Fig.	• Label used to recall a recurring accompaniment pattern (usually chordal).
Riff	• Label used to recall composed, melodic lines (usually single notes) which recur.
Fill	• Label used to identify a brief melodic figure which is to be inserted into the arrangement.
Rhy. Fill	• A chordal version of a Fill.
tacet	• Instrument is silent (drops out).

D.S. al Coda • Go back to the sign (𝄋), then play until the measure marked "***To Coda***," then skip to the section labelled "**Coda**."

D.C. al Fine • Go back to the beginning of the song and play until the measure marked "***Fine***" (end).

• Repeat measures between signs.

• When a repeated section has different endings, play the first ending only the first time and the second ending only the second time.

NOTE: Tablature numbers in parentheses mean:
    1. The note is being sustained over a system (note in standard notation is tied), or
    2. The note is sustained, but a new articulation (such as a hammer-on, pull-off, slide or vibrato) begins, or
    3. The note is a barely audible "ghost" note (note in standard notation is also in parentheses).